James Morton

Chrysanthemum Culture for America

A Book about Chrysanthemums, their History, Classification and Care

James Morton

Chrysanthemum Culture for America
A Book about Chrysanthemums, their History, Classification and Care

ISBN/EAN: 9783337176631

Printed in Europe, USA, Canada, Australia, Japan

Cover: Foto ©ninafisch / pixelio.de

More available books at **www.hansebooks.com**

RURAL LIBRARY SERIES

CHRYSANTHEMUM CULTURE

FOR AMERICA

A Book about Chrysanthemums, their History,
Classification and Care

BY

JAMES MORTON

Author of

SOUTHERN FLORICULTURE

1891

THE RURAL PUBLISHING COMPANY

TIMES BUILDING, NEW YORK

PREFACE.

TO ALL who cultivate the Chrysanthemum—the Star-eyed Daughter of the Fall—the author presents this little volume that he has endeavored to make replete with tidings of the Autumn Queen.

Numerous works have been devoted to this favorite flower, but they are chiefly of English origin, and in view of the great difference in our climatic conditions, they can only with uncertainty be adopted as guides in our country. There have also been issued a few excellent treatises on the Chrysanthemum, that except in a casual manner do not deal with anything further than mere cultural details, and it is therefore hoped that the ensuing pages will be of interest to those who are desirous of obtaining, in addition to cultural instructions, a brief history of their favorite flower, gleaned from many sources.

The wonderful progress in the culture of the Chrysanthemum under the influences of American environments, the matchless beauty and vigor of the American seedlings, together with the all-important demand for information regarding its culture, have suggested the publication of the present volume, presenting the results of experience gained beneath American skies and enumerating the varieties most popular among American amateur and professional florists.

It is also hoped that the present volume will prove companionable, and gain admission into the fellowship of works devoted to our Queen by other growers who have written of their favorite flower and mine, and that it may find for itself an abiding place in the hearts and homes of all people.

In regard to a large portion of the historical matter presented, the writer desires to express his obligations and gratitude for the kindly assistance of that profound student of chrysanthemum history, Mr. C. Harman Payne, of London, England. He would also acknowledge his indebtedness to the pages of the *Gardener's Magazine*, and to Mr. Shirley Hibberd,* its courteous and learned conductor.

Clarksville, Tenn.   JAMES MORTON.

---

*The author is pained to learn, since this volume has been in press, of the death of this revered horticultural leader.

CONTENTS.

THE RURAL NEW-YORKER.
THE AMERICAN GARDEN.
OUT-DOOR BOOKS.

CHAPTER I.

___   ___

Oriental and European History.

FROM almost pre-historic times the inhabitants of China and Japan have cultivated this famous flower with a wonderful devotion. From the earliest times travelers have related the esteem in which this plant was held by the inhabitants of the flowery kingdom. The propitious climate enabled the gardeners to display its virtues and advance its fame until it now adorns the humblest cottage as well as the habitation of the exalted mandarin. This great love for the chrysanthemum in the Celestial Empire, as well as in the Mikado's kingdom, did not extend to the entire genus, but was confined to the varieties indigenous to their climate, toward which they still exhibit the most ardent and unchanging admiration.

The chrysanthemum derives its name from the Greek words, *chrysos*, gold, and *anthos*, a flower, the literal meaning, therefore, being "gold flower," and in such varieties as Grandiflorum, Gold, and a host of others, the petals are of a rich, golden yellow, which abundantly justifies the name. It is an extensive genus of composite plants, and includes species which are to be found growing in nearly every part of the world, some of them being so far remote as the extreme northeast of Asia, while many others are indigenous to various parts of western Europe. In Asia the barren steppes of

Siberia are the habitat of *C. absinthifolium*, and Kamtchatka that
of *C. carinatum*.   In northern Africa are found *C. paludosum*,
C. carinatum and *C. pumilum ;* in Asiatic Turkey, *C. tanaceti-
folium* and *C. lancifolium ;* in Hungary, *C. rotundifolium* and *C.
sylvestre ;* in Austria, *C. atratum ;* in Spain, *C. anomalum* and
C. radicans, and in France, *C. montanum* and *C. perpusillum.*
Great Britain has *C. Leucanthemum*, the ox-eye daisy, and *C.
segetum*, the corn marigold, which are also found in America,
all belonging to the same family.   Notwithstanding the long
list given, it will be observed that it is not by any means complete, inasmuch as Russia, Switzerland, Italy, Sicily, the
Levant, Mexico, India, China and Japan contribute additional
species of this important and widespread genus.   But of all
these species, those of India, China, and Japan are perhaps
the most usually denoted by the comprehensive word—chrysanthemum—among the majority of people who are engaged
in the cultivation of this beautiful and deservedly popular
autumn flower, the named varieties of which alone already
number between two and three thousand, and are constantly
increasing.

There are good reasons for supposing that it was cultivated
with much devotion by the gardeners of China and Japan for
centuries before its importation into Europe.   A well-known
traveler in those countries tells us in one of his works that
"so great a favorite is the chrysanthemum with the Chinese
gardeners that no persuasion will deter them from its culture,
and they will frequently resign their situations rather than be
forbidden by their employers to grow it."   In support of this
statement, he relates the experience of an English resident in
that country, who, without the slightest interest in the plant,
was compelled to allow his native gardener the pleasure of
cultivating it solely on that account.   The Chinese often train
the chrysanthemum into curious and fantastic forms, such as
pagodas, horses, stags, ships, etc.   Another peculiar method

of culture practiced at Chea-yuen, where it is extensively cultivated, is the grafting of cuttings into stout stems of *Artemisia indica* as a stock. Among the Japanese the chrysanthemum is no less prized than in China, and they display great skill in its culture, calling it the Queen of Flowers. At the most popular of the Japanese festivals, the people display effigies of their traditional heroes, constructed of massive chrysanthemum blossoms, Benkei, the Japanese Hercules, appearing gorgeously appareled in white, yellow and purple pompons.

In many other ways the Chinese and Japanese reveal their love for this plant, but probably in no more apparent and lasting manner than by applying the talent of their most skillful artists to portray its fair form and vivid coloring on their pottery and household fabrics, as well as in numberless illustrated books and pamphlets.

In Japan the Imperial Order of the Chrysanthemum is the most distinguished decoration of the Empire. It was founded in 1876, and consists of a star and collar hung around the neck by a riband, the whole work being in gold, silver and enamels. Bestowed, with rare exceptions, only upon royal personages, it is consequently considered a very high distinction among European sovereigns who have been wearers of this mark of the Mikado's favor. The chrysanthemum, or "kiku," as it is called in Japan, is also one of the crest badges of the imperial family, and is used as an official seal. The hilts of the swords forged by the Emperor Go Toba, who ascended the throne in 1186, had the kiku figured upon them.

The chrysanthemum season in Japan is looked forward to with much pleasure, and the different communities manifest the greatest enthusiasm in its culture. A certain day is set apart as a festival, when all turn out to pay due homage to their national emblem, the many-hued chrysanthemum. During their blooming period the gardens of all the prominent florists present an exhibition of great beauty. Each evening for many weeks the notables of rank, as well as the peasants in holiday attire, join in the happy festivities. The fetes are always held in the evenings and the grounds are beautifully illuminated, presenting a scene brilliant beyond description. His Majesty also opens his gardens at the Imperial Palace on this grand fete day. All the highest native officials and foreign residents of distinction are present, and invitations are highly prized and much sought after. It is one of the few occasions when the Empress is to be seen in public. She delights in having the most dainty handkerchiefs of gauze embroidered in chrysanthemums of all colors. Her ladies of honor also appear in gorgeous dresses with chrysanthemums worked upon them. Upon this occasion the display of the national flower is said to be unequaled. Nowhere can they be found in such profusion, so fully developed and brilliant in color, while the rich imperial violet silk with which the tents and buildings are draped bear upon them the heraldic kiku in all its pristine loveliness. As the day draws to a close the people return to their homes to complete the slow process of intoxication by drinking saki, into which are thrown the blooms of chrysanthemums, which they suppose will preserve them from evil the coming year.

The varieties cultivated in Japan are numerous, many of them having exquisite beauty, as the importations of late years attest. True, they may not have Ada Spaulding, Mrs. Carnegie, Mrs. W. K. Harris, or any of the American prize winners, but we believe their wealth of beautiful sorts is yet far from exhausted, and we may expect in the not distant future, through the indomitable enterprise of the American importer, to have representatives of all the most desirable sorts now grown by our Japanese friends blossoming in exhibition halls of our American cities. Judging from the new type of chrysanthemums of which Mrs. Alpheus Hardy and Louis Boehmer are forerunners in the United States, we can-

not but think that, with the combined efforts of the importer
and the hybridizer, its varieties will, within the next decade,
be augmented many fold.　The varieties with soft, feathery
growth, over which so much ado has been made within the
past few years, have long been common in Japan, for Mr.
Fortune tried many years since to bring to England a variety
that had its florets edged very beautifully with a hair-like
fringe, but it was unfortunately lost on the way.　The chrysanthemums in Japan are not confined to the autumn varieties,
for several beautiful summer blooming kinds of large size are
to be met with in the gardens of that country.　These, however, would never become as popular in our climate as the
fall flowering varieties, as the season of blooming has much
to do with the popularity of the many varieties we cultivate.
What is known as the umbelliferous chrysanthemums have
not made much progress among our florists as yet.　These
varieties are grown in the southern province, Kiushiu, and,
though the flowers are small, their branches are very compact,
forming a plant a yard in diameter.

We have been taught that there is no such thing in nature
as plants of the same species producing scarlet, yellow and
blue flowers.　Perhaps the nearest approach to this is the
hyacinth, but in this, although we have the yellow and blue,
we have no true scarlet.　Neither is there any true scarlet
among the chrysanthemums, which encourages some credence
in the information regarding the existence in Japan of a
variety with blue flowers.　In the "History of Nin-toku-ten-
wan" the following passage occurs : "In 386, in the seventy-
third year of his reign, seeds of the chrysanthemum were
first introduced into Japan from a foreign country, both blue
and yellow, red, white and violet."　There are frequently
represented on Japanese porcelain, both ancient and modern,
especially that of Satsuma and Kioto, chrysanthemum blossoms in blue or emerald green, to which fact may be attriLuted

the notion that a blue chrysanthemum exists in Japan. It is supposed to be in the possession of the Japanese Buddhist priests, who guard it with jealous care from the eyes of western travelers, and refuse to allow it to leave their hands. M. Em. Rodigrez, the well-known Belgian horticulturist, writing upon this subject, says : "Some day, perhaps, we shall get a sight of this famous blue chrysanthemum, which we are assured exists somewhere in the Celestial Empire, but which has been sought for in vain. It may grow in the valley of the King-Chang-Oola, inaccessable to Europeans and Americans, as is also the blue camellia, and the blue lily."

Beside the potter, metal worker, weaver and ivory carver, the painter also has lavished his skill on this charming flower. In common with the cherry blossom and convolvulus, the chryanthemum enjoys the distinction of having illustrated books concerning it, specially designed by talented artists, and many a renowned artist has not disdained it as the subject of his masterpiece.

The name of the ninth month in Japan, in which the kiku is in bloom, is Kiku-dzuki, and on the ninth day of Kiku-dzuki the principal festivals of the country are held, when mirth and feasting are the order of the day. The commonest girl's name in Japan is O-kiku San, which means Honorable Miss Chrysanthemum.

It is nearly two hundred years since this plant first became known in Europe. It was at various times mentioned by many of the early botanists under different names, but they disagreed as to the genus with which it should be classed. Bregnius in 1689 most accurately describes the Chinese varieties, and was first to mention the species, calling it *Matricaria Japonica maxima*, giving it also the Japanese name "kychonophane." He makes allusion to six distinct varieties, white, blush, rose, yellow, purple and crimson, which he says were growing in Holland at that time. These plants were subsequently lost in the Dutch gardens, and it is strange that no account of them can be discovered, and that the gardeners of Holland knew nothing of them when the chrysanthemum was again introduced into Europe a century later. The next mention of the chrysanthemum is in 1690, by Rheede, a Dutch scientist, in which he alleges that the Dutch were the first Europeans to cultivate the small-flowered varieties, and that it was taken by them to their distant colonies of Amboyna and Malabar, where the name of "tsjettipu" was given it. Plukenet describes the small-flowered plants under the name *Matricaria Sinensis*, describing what is thought to be the Chinese chrysanthemum *Matricaria Japonica maxima*, referring also to the kychonophane of Bregnius.

The learned Engelbert Kæmpfer, who visited Japan in 1690, describes the Chinese chrysanthemum, under the name matricaria, as growing wild in the gardens, being called by the natives kik, kikf, or kikku. He says that there are many varieties, some of which are in blossom at all seasons of the year, and that they are the principal ornaments of all the gardens. Rumphius, in the year 1750, gives a description of plants collected in Amboyna and the adjacent islands, in which the small flowered species is described as *Matricaria Sinensis*, and is said to have been introduced from China. He also states that in the latter country it is cultivated in pots, and that the Chinese gardeners keep it dwarf and allow only one bloom upon a shoot.

It appears in the "Hortus Kewensis" that in England the first known plant of the chrysanthemum which bore a small yellow blossom, was growing in the Apothecarius Botanic Garden at Chelsea in 1764, but was at that time little esteemed and soon lost sight of. A fortunate circumstance, bearing upon this history, is that when Sir Thomas Sloan conveyed the land forming this garden to the Apothecarius Society in 1722, he inserted in the covenant a clause binding them to present to the Royal Society fifty dried specimens of distinct plants every year until the number reached two thousand. In accordance, therefore, with the terms of the deed, a specimen of this small yellow variety was, with other plants, presented by the society's gardener, Phillip Miller, to the Royal Society under the name *Matricaria indica*, and is still preserved in the British Museum.

Thunberg, in his " Flora Japonica," describes the plant in 1784, which he asserts is Linnæus's *C. indicum*, and refers to the preceding account by Kæmpfer. He, too, gives the Japanese appellations, kik, kikf, kikku, kikof, and kiko-no fanna, which latter name is but a different form of the word kychonophane, used by Bregnius, the word fanna being used by the Japanese as expressive of elegance. Thunberg mentions a great difference in color as well as size, also single and double flowering kinds, all of which are grown in the gardens of Japan on account of their beautiful flowers produced in the autumn months, and he tells us that it is the same plant mentioned by Kæmpfer as matricaria.

Loureiro, the Portugese traveler, in his account in 1790 of the plants of Cochin China, refers to the *C. indicum* of Linnæus, but his description evidently belongs to the Chinese chrysanthemum. He speaks of the variety of the color of its flowers, which he states are white, red, blush, yellow, violet and purple, of various sizes, and grown in all the gardens of China and Cochin China.

Ramatuella calls it *Anthemis grandiflora*, while Willdenow, in 1801, placed it under the same genus, but gave it another specific name, calling it *Anthemis artemisiæfolia*. Among other botanical writers who described it, may be mentioned Moench, Ray, Swett, Morrison, Valliant, Persoon and Desfontaines.

Thus, while the chrysanthemum culture of to-day is denominated a modern craze, it was in olden times the object of more than ordinary interest.

It will be seen that up to this time a great diversity of opinion existed among botanists as to its true generic and specific name. The writings of Joseph Sabine afford much useful and interesting information regarding the diversity of opinion as to which genus the large-flowering or Chinese chrysanthemum belongs. He contended that the varieties then known were not the *C. indicum* of Linnæus. In his exhaustive papers he gave an account of his study and research, definitely setting the whole matter at rest, the result being that the small-flowered varieties were *C. indicum*, whereas the large Chinese chrysanthemum of 1789, and its successors, were proved by him to belong to an entirely different species, thenceforth to be known as *C. Sinensis.*

The chrysanthemum, up to 1824, was distinguished only by its form and color. The Chinese names, many of which were curious and fanciful, could only be applied with uncertainty. The following, translated from the original by Mr. Reeves, will serve as examples of the names by which the chrysanthemum was known in the Celestial Empire : "The purple lily, the white wave of autumn, the purple peasant's tail, the scarlet robe, the yellow gold thread, the purple butterfly, the purple peasant's feather, the yellow tiger's claw, the crystal wave and the drunken lady."

The Japanese also, in bestowing names, follow the example of their neighbors, and it is not unusual to find them exhibiting varieties labeled with such names as "Mountain Mist," "Autumnal Cloud," and "Ten thousand times sprinkled with gold."

A few years afterwards, as soon as the French and Dutch started in a sort of floral hero worship, a new system of nomenclature was brought into existence by naming the plants after the principal celebrities in their respective countries. In 1827 a writer in "Hone's Table Book," under the heading of "Winter Flowers," refers undoubtedly to the chrysanthemum, and adopts the pseudonym of "Jerry Blossoms." The writer also stated that there was little chance for its ripening seed, as it bloomed at the commencement of winter. Mr. Sabine was also of the same opinion, and up to this time no chrysanthemums had been produced from seed in England. We are told by Mr. Burbidge, in his very excellent work upon chrysanthemums, that about that year Isaac Wheeler, gardener and porter of Magdalen Hall, now Hertford College, Oxford, raised the first English seedlings; and on December 2d, 1832, Mr. Wheeler exhibited some of his seedlings in London, and received a silver Banksian medal for them as the earliest chrysanthemums raised in England. They were insignificant blooms compared with those of the present day, and were referred to only as a curiosity. In 1835 some seedlings were raised in Norfolk, which Mr. Salter claims were the first ever produced in England. These were grown by Mr. Short and Mr. Freestone. The latter was the more successful grower, as some varieties raised at that time exist to the present day.

It is a noteworthy fact, in connection with the chrysanthemum, that the interest in the flower has never been allowed to abate. At several periods of its existence some unexpected development, or departure from the ordinary course, has given new impetus to its cultivation, and excited the curiosity and admiration of its growers, when it might have otherwise ceased to retain its hold upon their affections. In the year 1846 an instance of this occurred in England, when the small-flowered species known as pompon was introduced. In 1843 the Horticultural Society of London sent Robert Fortune, the superintendent of the glass department of their garden, to China, and, on his return in 1846, he brought home, with other curiosities, two small-flowered varieties, known as Chusan Daisy. These were at once introduced into the Versailles nursery and soon became favorites with the French, their seedlings being more double than the original. From their compactness and resemblance to a rosette, they received the name of pompons. Mr. Salter and Mr. Fortune both say, and they are probably right, that from those two varieties all the pompons now in cultivation sprung.

Yet another, and unquestionably the greatest impulse, was given in 1860–61, by this same determined collector, when, on his second journey to the far East, he sent to England seven varieties much esteemed by the florists of Japan, which created almost a revolution in the chrysanthemum world at that time, and they are to-day by far the most popular sorts grown upon the American and European continents. Among those first sent out, and which still remain among the best, are Grandiflorum, Baron de Prailly, Yellow Dragon and Hero of Magdala.

During all the time the chrysanthemum was making such rapid strides, and fast taking its place as a favorite flower in England, it made little progress in France, to a native of which its first introduction was due. A year after Blanchard's importation it was grown in the Jardin des Plantes, but, like the variety of Chelsea, was but little appreciated, and nearly received a similar fate. Thirty-six years after the old purple variety reached the shores of France, there were not more than fifteen varieties cultivated, and these of no particular merit either in form or color. Few French florists at that period were interested in its culture, and consequently we should give due credit to the English for first appreciating its value as an autumn flower, and giving it so prominent a position in its early days.

This treatment by the French, however, was not universal, for Monsieur Noisette, who visited England in 1824, was presented with twenty-seven varieties from the gardens of the horticultural society. Another distinguished lover of horticulture, having thrown down the sword for the trowel and

hoe had grown chrysanthemums for some years prior to that
date.   This man, the celebrated Captain Bernet, was without
doubt the first person in Europe to raise the chrysanthemum
from seed, having produced several fine varieties in the year
1827.   Encouraged by his first success, which attached him
more and more to his favorite plants, he saw his collection
annually increase by the addition of many new varieties.
Three years after this event an experienced nurseryman got
possession of an entire set of Captain Bernet's new chrysanthemums, and propagated them for sale.   Thus it was from
1830 to 1836 that his novelties were disseminated among the
plant dealers in Paris and abroad.   The French chrysanthemum growers are still very proud of Captain Bernet's
achievements with their favorite plant, and dub him with the
Washingtonian appellation of "Father of the Chrysanthemum."   There still remain in commerce a few of the varieties raised by him, but they are grown more as heirlooms than
for any value they possess, being catalogued only by a florist
who claims to be a grandson of Captain Bernet's old gardener.

For the past twenty-five years those French florists who
have taken up the culture of the chrysanthemum have been
working at their improvement steadily and surely.   They have
not only produced varieties greatly superior to any of their
early sorts, but they have been instrumental in producing varieties which, in brilliancy of color, may be said to be unpar-
alleled.

The most prominent growers in France of late years are
Simon Delaux, M. de Reydellet, Dr. Audiguer, the producer of
Soliel Levant ; Mons. F. Marranch, Mons. J. M. Pigny, Dr.
Barrie ; Victor Lemoine, who raised Fulgore, several pompons
and large flowering varieties ; Mons. Boulanger, who sent out
Gloria de Mazaryue and several other sorts not generally
grown in this country, and Mons. Bernard, who sent out
Gloria Rayonnante, M. Fremy, Reine Margot, and who also

produced a few pompons; Mons. Boucharlat, noted principally for his pompons, which belonged chiefly to the lilliputian
class; Mons. Lacroix—not to be confounded with an amateur
of the same name—a comparatively recent grower, whose best
known flowers are Parasol, M'd'lle Lacroix, Flocon de Neige,
Jeanne d'Arc and Fabias de Mediana; Mons. Marrouch, to
whom we are indebted for Madame Clemence Audiguer, Mar-
guerite Marrouch, Mons. Marrouch, Madame Clos and others;
Mons. Pertuzes, whose flowers are not very well known in
America, except Timbal de Argent and Triumph de la Rue
des Chalets.

In the year 1850, so far as we can learn, those little gems,
the anemone pompons, were first shown. The first were
Eucharis, Medee, and Thisbe, all being distributed by M.
Bonamay, of Toulouse.

The most eminent of all the French growers is Mons. Simon
Delaux, St. Martin du Tauch, near Toulouse, whose successes
have been most brilliantly exhibited in the Japanese varieties,
and to him the author is deeply indebted for much valuable
information regarding his favorite flower in the sunny land of
France. The name of Delaux is a guaranty of merit in a
chrysanthemum, and his productions are admired and cultivated upon both hemispheres. Such varieties as Tokio, M.
Boyer, Royal Aquarium, Rose Laing, Bouquet Fait, Eclatarete,
Jeanne Delaux, Mons. Tarin, will long perpetuate the mem-
ory of this noted cultivator. It is difficult to find, at any of
our exhibitions, the smallest stand of cut blooms or collection
of plants that does not contain some originated by this eminent florist. Mons. de Reydellet ranks second to his great
rival and fellow-countryman, M. Delaux. Mons. Reydellet is
not a professional florist, but an amateur grower of new seedlings, La Triumphant and Marsa being two which are well
known in America.

To American growers it will seem strange that such a thing

as a chrysanthemum society does not exist in France. We quote from a letter of Messrs. Lemoine and Fils, Nancy, dated July 9, 1890, in which they kindly give the following information : "We have no chrysanthemum society in France, but the numerous horticultural societies in our country are much interested in chrysanthemums, and nearly every one has a chrysanthemum show at the proper season. Pot-grown plants are generally exhibited ; cut flowers in small quantities only. Here we do not grow the specimens for exhibition, as the practice is in England and America. We do not care for the enormous flowers that English florists obtain, or huge plants with only a few blooms upon them. Here the plants are treated to give the largest number of blooms, and in the most natural way. New varieties of chrysanthemums are not very largely produced in France, except in the southern portions. Here in Nancy we have a severe climate, and it is nearly impossible to get seeds of the double varieties. Personally, we have sent out some good novelties, but the seed that yielded them was not our own. There is no country where there is so large a quantity of novelties raised annually as in France. For instance, this year, Simon Delaux, of Tolouse, offers 24 new varieties of his own production ; M. de Reydellet, of Valance, 18 novelties ; M. Louis Lacroix, 25 varieties ; M. Rozain Boucharlet, of Lyons, 14 novelties ; M. Host, of Lyons, 7- novelties ; M. Santel, of Salon, near Marseilles, 12 novelties, besides a number raised by Etienne Lacroix, M. Bernard, Pertuzes and Audiguer, of Tolouse, and others. Over two hundred novelties are annually produced in the south of France, principally of the Japanese and Chinese forms."

From this we note that the large blooms and specimens of plants so common at our shows here are not seen in France, and, judging from the schedule of prizes of some of the different exhibitions at hand, their culture is not encouraged. The arrangement of plants for the best effect is one of the leading points in the award of premiums. The French seem also particularly partial to the Japanese varieties, and ever since their introduction by Mr. Robert Fortune, they have excited a great interest among the florists. From 1870 to 1880 there were but few incurved flowers distributed from France, and at that time it seemed as if they would excel all other countries in the production of the Japanese varieties. Happily, however, in our own climate, a Thorpe a Walcott, a Harris, and a Spaulding have supplied our need, and the production of these men is eminently satisfactory to the American cultivator. It will, however, be many years even if no further advance be made by the French, before their contribution to our collections will play an insignificant part in our gardens and exhibition halls.

One great objection, frequently, and not without reason, advanced against the French productions, is that they are far too numerous to be uniformly good, thus incurring a waste of time and money to those who distribute them in England and America. It is to be regretted, too, that the French taste, though refined, differs from us somewhat in floriculture. Had their energies been turned more to specimen plants and exhibition blooms, or had they learned to appreciate the value of the incurved section, it is difficult to imagine how great would have been the results in these directions. They have, notwithstanding these ideas, given us a new type, and one capable of considerable development—the Japanese anemone, a result of intelligent crossing. M. Marrauch, who died a few years ago, was one of the successful producers of this new class. They are at present wanting in high tones of color, compared with their congeners of the common Japanese type, but their number is steadily increasing, and if duly appreciated greater results may be attained. Several new growers have of late come into notice in France, and we shall probably hear more from their labors in the future, as their enthusiasm in the culture of the chrysanthemum meets with its due reward.

In the year 1779 M. Blanchard, a merchant of Marseilles, imported three plants frem China, but out of these three only one—a purple flower—reached France alive.   This is the one of which Ramatuelle published an account, calling it, as previously quoted, *Anthemis grandiflora*, having satisfied himself and the French botanists that it could not be the *C. indicum* of Linnæus.   In the following year M. Cels, a Parisian nurseryman of considerable repute, sent to the Royal Gardens at Kew what was the first large-flowering chrysanthemum in modern times, known either in England or on the continent. In November, 1795, it bloomed at Chelsea, at the nursery of Messrs. Colville, a firm much noted in after years for the beauty of their chrysanthemums.   No other variety was known for several years, until 1798, when between that year and 1808, eight new varieties were imported, one by Mr. Thomas Evans of Stepheny, and the remaining seven by Sir Abraham Hume. To these nine varieties a tenth was added, namely the changeable white, a sport from the old purple of 1802.   In 1798, the rose and buff were introduced ; in 1802, the golden yellow, and the sulphur yellow ; in 1806, the Spanish brown ; in 1808, the quilled white and the large lilac.   Of these the sulphur yellow was the one imported by Mr. Evans, and the other seven were imported through the agency of Sir A. Hume.

Between the years 1808 and 1816, there was another suspension of importations, but in the latter year and up to 1823 there were several new varieties introduced.   For the first few decades in the present century there was scarcely any plant half so popular as the Chinese chrysanthemum, and as it had then attracted considerable attention and become a favorite flower it began to sell for a high price.   The Messrs. Colville, who were the first to succeed in producing blooms of the purple chrysanthemum—which it may be easily imagined have little resemblance to those we see at the present time—were as proud of their success at that period as if they had raised a Cullingfordii or a Violet Rose. The interest of the zealous gardeners of England having now been excited, they were induced to continue the introduction of additional sorts. Mr. John Reeves, a tea buyer for the East India Company, in addition to the two gentlemen already named, was among the most active men in enlarging the list. About this period others began to take an interest, and Mr. Reeves, who acted as a correspondent at Canton of the Horticultural Society, sent to England in 1820 twelve kinds, so that the next year opened with good prospects for those whose interest had been the cause of their advent. In the autumn of that year twelve varieties, all whose habits and character of flowers were then ascertained, were grown in the gardens of the Horticultural Society of London. Aided by the friendly exertions of Mr. Reeves and the commanders of the China ships, new varieties were continually being brought to England, though unfortunately many entire consignments were lost on the way. At the beginning of 1824, twenty-seven well known sorts which had been thoroughly tested and approved, had been represented in various botanical works. In 1826 the Horticultural Society's collection comprised forty-eight distinct kinds, four of which were sports which originated in England.

During the year 1824, Mr. Parks, who was sent to China by the Horticultural Society, forwarded many varieties to England at different times, among which was the Yellow Waratah, a variety entirely different from all the others, and supposed to be the precursor of the large-flowered anemone section. Up to this date eighteen sorts had been engraved in works like the *Botanical Magazine* and the *Botanical Register*, but with the exception of one or two, they have gradually disappeared. Donald Monroe, gardener to the Horticultural Society some years later, gives a list of forty-nine distinct sorts of the Chinese varieties, enumerating all the sorts to which allusion has been made. In the autumn of 1825 a brilliant display of chrysanthemums was held in the Horticultural Society's garden at Chiswick, through the exertion of its devoted secretary, Mr. Sabine. Pot grown plants to the number of seven hundred, were in flower on that occasion. This display gave a great impetus to its cultivation, so that from this period the people became fully awake to the beauty and usefulness of the chrysanthemum, as an invaluable autumn flower.

Among those who in after years developed the chrysanthemum in England, the name of Samuel Broome stands pre-eminent. In 1832 he obtained employment as gardener at the Inner Temple, and gave much attention to the chrysanthemum, his annual display acquiring a world-wide reputation. He also published a book, " Culture of the Chrysanthemum," in 1857, which was many times reprinted, and is still worthy of respect for its sound teachings, and should be on the shelf of every chrysanthemum grower.

The first chrysanthemum exhibition in England was held in Birmingham in 1836, of which there is but little record. In 1843 the people of Norwich also inaugurated a chrysanthemum show, but it was not until three years later that the first chrysanthemum society of importance was formed.

In an old fashioned hostelry known as the " Rochester Castle," in a rural suburb of Stoke Newington, where the tradesmen loved to gather every evening, a chrysanthemum association was formed, which was the first to endure to the present day. Mr. Robert James, landlord of the " Rochester," a first rate host, an able florist and a man of broad sympathies, had made chrysanthemums his favorites, and had at that time a collection of twenty-five sorts that he cared for as pets and of which he was very proud. The talk at the inn turned to floriculture, as it often did, and an exhibition of chrysanthe-

mums was determined upon, Robert James leading the move-
ment as treasurer and advocate ; and he was ever known as
father of the first chrysanthemum show. This association
was known as the Stoke Newington, later the Borough of
Hackney Florists' Society, and still more recently, the National
Chrysanthemum Society. For many years it prospered under
its original name, which was afterwards discarded for that of
the Borough of Hackney. Owing to the large number of new
members, and to extend the sphere of the society's work, it
was finally given the name of the National Chrysanthemum
Society. This society, in addition to the usual November
show, now holds each year exhibitions of early flowering
chrysanthemums, as well as conducting exhibitions in the
chief provincial cities. The society's official catalogue is
accepted as the standard for all questions of classification and
nomenclature, and is an excellent book of reference for chrysanthemum growers in either England or America.

As if by magic every important town in England followed
this example, and at the present time nearly every town and
village has its chrysanthemum show.

Mr. John Salter also did much to advance the interest of
the autumn queen in England, his name being to the present
day most pleasantly associated with the chrysanthemum and
familiar to growers on both sides of the Atlantic. He first
commenced his horticultural career as an amateur at Shep-
herd's Bush, near London, but afterwards removed to Versailles, France, where the climate was more congenial to the
cultivation of his favorite flower. He was personally ac-
quainted with many of the French and other growers and
knew far more of the progress of foreign growers than any
man in England in his day. His work "The Chrysanthemum, Its History and Culture," published twenty-five years
ago, is still, notwithstanding its age, a book of much value.
From it we learn that, finding the climate of France more

suitable for the purpose of raising seedling chrysanthemums, Mr. Salter went to Versailles in 1838 for the purpose of establishing a nursery to enable him to accomplish his design. He imported from England most of the Jersey and Norfolk seedlings, to which he added 250 of the best French sorts, so that in 1840 the number of varieties he had in cultivation amounted to between 300 and 400. Five years after his establishment in France, Mr. Salter produced his first seedling, "Annie Salter," in the nursery at Versailles, which he sent out in 1844, and which is well known at the present time. In 1847 the "Queen of England" followed, which is considered a good variety to-day, although forty years old. The French revolution of 1848, with its social changes, necessitated Mr. Salter's return to his native land, where he died in 1874.

Up to 1865 the influx of the new varieties of incurved, reflexed, and large anemone flowers continued, and many of our favorites appeared at the date, viz: Cherub, John Salter, Lady Slade, Nil Desperandum, White Christine, Cleopatra and others. The chrysanthemum was now probably a more popular flower than ever. Societies had sprung up all over the country, and during November the exhibitions were thronged by thousands of admirers. Some years elapsed after the introduction of the Japanese sorts before they became common, or before seedlings were raised from the new varieties. They were, however, not much admired by old school florists, who contemptuously dubbed them "ragged jacks," on account of their curious forms and irregular petals. It is believed that those originally introduced were Grandiflorum, Golden Dragon, Bronze Dragon, Striatum, Laciniatum and Roseum Punctatum. One of these died on the way, but was afterwards reproduced from seed of the survivors. Previous to the year 1866, no seedlings were distributed from the Japanese sorts, and probably the first of them were Aurantium, Countess de Boregard, Gold Thread, Mad. Godilott, Tarantula, and

Tycoon. The varieties belonging to this section were in those days rather inclined to be later bloomers than the chrysanthemums generally grown. By some they were looked upon as likely to be serviceable for conservatory decoration, but fit for nothing else, as their defiance of all canons of good taste placed them quite beyond the pale of .a flower show ; and there were not a few who regarded them as veritable abominations, judged by the chrysanthemum fancy then in vogue.

Now that the present generation have become accustomed to the fantastic form of these wonderful floral triumphs, and their brilliancy of color, to which the chrysanthemum owes much of its popularity at the present day, it is amusing to read what was prophesied about them twenty-three years ago. A correspondent in the *Florist and Pomologist* in 1866 says : "I fear that the new Japanese flowers recently introduced by Mr. Fortune will scarcely become favorites with any of us. They are loose, ungainly looking things, with colors by no means attractive, and the less said about their form the better. They may possibly be turned by-and-by to account by the hybridizers ; but as a class, unless there can be some very marked improvements in them, they will soon be discarded."

What has been the result ? Out of the original seven, five have remained in cultivation to the present day, and two of these, Grandiflorum and Golden Dragon, rank among the best that have been produced since. In view of such a revolution as this, prophetic words for the future must be given with a due regard to the fickle tastes of the public.

In 1866, Mr. George Glenny, writing of form in the chrysanthemum, says : "The flower ought in form to be one-half or two-thirds of a sphere, the center compact and outline round, the whole face symmetrical and close, and the petals free from notches at the end. The reflexed petal is inferior to the cupped or incurved, but if the flower be of proper form when

shown it loses only one point." Such was the standard of
excellence in the "good old times" for a chrysanthemum, but
now it is far removed from what Mr. Glenny describes as his
ideal. In England, however, the incurved and reflexed varieties are still justly popular, but with us the "Jap" is still
supreme. We will not attempt to peer into the future ; popular taste is too inconstant, and the successful grower who
would see the chrysanthemum maintain its present foremost
position must be ever ready to avail himself of new ideas in
seeding, growing and showing, and attracting public attention in some way to the beauty and usefulness of the flower.

In 1881, Messrs. Veitch & Sons of London imported from
Japan six new sorts, called Ben d' Or, Comte de Germiny,
Duchess of Connaught, Thunberg, and others, all of which are
well known. Messrs. Mahood & Son were also successful in
raising some very fine seedlings in England, as were Mr. Run-
dle, Mr. Bull, Mr. Cullingford, Mr. N. Davis, Mr. George
Stevens, and Mr. Teedesdale, whose flowers can be found
described in any catalogue of chrysanthemums. The names
also of Joseph Dale, Isaac Wheeler, Edwin Merry, Robert
James, Adam Forsyth, George Taylor and George Glenny
will long be remembered in the chrysanthemum lore of England for their devotion to this favorite flower. Happily the
succeeding generation has produced men to take up their
labors, and the admirers of the autumn queen have suffered
little in the change. With such men as Mr. C. Harman
Payne, a master of the literature of the subject, and Mr.
Edwin Molyneaux, the champion grower of cut flowers, Mr.
Wm. Holmes, Mr. C. Ochard, and Mr. Robert Owen in the
lead, we may expect to see great results.

Considerable attention has also been given the chrysanthemum in the islands of the English Channel. In 1836 Mons.
Lebois, an amateur in Jersey, turned his attention to the raising of seedlings, and produced some marked improvements.

He was so extraordinarily fortunate in their cultivation that he raised upwards of five hundred seedlings, which he sold to Mr. Chandler, of the Vauxhall nurseries, and a considerable number of them were known twenty-five years ago.

According to a correspondent of Mr. Burbridge, the producer of the first seedlings in the Channel Islands, was a baker, and had his plants trained to the wall behind the oven. Others soon followed, among them Messrs. Clarke, Davis, Pethers, Smith and Wolsley, while in latter years, Mr. Dawnton and Major Carey have contributed some very favorite sorts. In Mr. Salter's catalogue of chrysanthemums more than half appeared to be of Guernsey and Jersey origin. Our friends in the Channel Islands have done but little in recent years, compared with their former efforts, in raising new seedlings, although it is not entirely neglected. Mr. Smith has long since discontinued the growing of chrysanthemums from seed. Mr. Pethers, who went to the Cape of Good Hope, seemed not to have resumed its culture upon his return, and Mr. Clarke has been dead for several years. Mr. Davis, whose name is deserving of more than a passing notice from having obtained Prince Alfred, Prince of Wales and Princess of Wales, no longer devotes himself to the work. Mr. James Dawnton, the raiser of Elaine and Fair Maid of Guernsey, will be longest remembered of the Channel Island growers. Notwithstanding the lull in seedling growing at present, the chrysanthemum still has many friends and cultivators in these islands. Their first exhibition was held in 1865.

Belgium had its first chrysanthemum show in the autumn of 1866, which was organized by the Royal Agricultural Society of Ghent, and has been repeated in succeeding years, others having followed at Liego, Antwerp, and Tournay.

It is a matter of some difficulty to trace the work of chrysanthemum culture in Germany, but it is safe to assume that it was of some importance there in 1832, and has, we believe, been steadily gaining in favor to the present time. It is not generally known that the first independent work on the chrysanthemum was written by a German, who had a collection of the new flowers, in which were comprised most, if not all, those in cultivation in England and France, all of which are carefully described.

Up to the year 1854 no universal standard of merit in the blooms was adopted, every one having his own peculiar ideas of a good flower. A standard at that time adopted by the Stoke Newington Chrysanthemum Society, which was the same as that suggested by Mr. Glenny.

CHAPTER II.

American History.

THUS far we have hurriedly glanced at the early history of the chrysanthemum in the far east, in England, in France and the Channel Islands, and now the author comes home to our own chrysanthemums, with all their profusion of beauty. Their size, form, and color are probably unequalled in their original home in the far east. They are so refined by crossing, and strengthened by climate and culture, that their superiority has been universally acknowledged. Never before during its history has the cultivator been able to produce anything as fine as the blooms that are now raised beneath American skies and shown in the exhibition halls of our large cities.

The climate of the northern states is more conducive to the growth of individual plants under the care of the diligent cultivator. More care has to be exercised through the long dry summers of the south to produce fine specimens, but as an out-door flower, adapted to the gardens of all, one must go to the southern states to see them in their wild and promiscuous beauty.

It must have been long after the landing of the Pilgrim fathers that the chrysanthemum reached our shores, after a checkered voyage from the far east, probably about the year

(31)

1810, perhaps earlier ; but at that time it obtained little attention, as its beauties were undeveloped and its praises unsung.
Its early history upon our continent is lost, and it is not possible to say with any certainty who first cultivated it in the
the new world.

What little antiquity we have in America in relation to the
chrysanthemum clusters around the classic precincts of " The
Hub," although if record could be found, the writer is confi-
dent that several old North and South Carolina, as well as
Virginia gardens, might justly dispute the claim, as we find
from "the oldest inhabitant" that a variety of the small yellow
chrysanthemum was common in each of those places eighty
years ago.   These points in the history of our favorite flower
must long remain a matter of conjecture, but that it has come,
and come to stay, is a matter long since past discussion.
Being cultivated in England in 1795, not a long period could
have elapsed before it became known in America.

The florists of our large eastern cities were always so active
in obtaining novelties from their eastern correspondents, that
it was doubtless but a few years from the time of its introduction into England until its roots were firmly planted in American soil.

For many years it obtained much less attention than in the
countries of the old world.   Within the past twenty years,
however, the popularity of the flower has advanced at a steady
rate until it is now supreme in the home garden, the exhibition hall and the conservatory.   With such a command of
climate as the American continent affords, the entire culture
has been thoroughly mastered, including the propagation by
seed.   Its wonderful development in the past ten years, in the
hands of American cultivators, is phenemonal for so brief a
period.   Though beginning so recently, we are rapidly becoming rivals of the countries in which it originated.

Ten years ago but few chrysanthemums were cultivated

here, and those were probably imported from England. Now all is changed, and importations from China and Japan are easily and frequently made, seedlings are raised the equal of any in the old world, and new kinds, as they appear, are introduced from Europe. Thus American chrysanthemum fanciers are supplied at the present day with each new and beautiful variety as soon as it appears regardless of the source from which it comes.

With such a wealth of charms, both native and exotic, annually unfolded before a people with whom beauty and merit are so quickly appreciated, it is not so surprising to find that the chrysanthemum has extended in a few years into every portion of our country. In all sections the chrysanthemum is now a reigning favorite, and American florists claim a fair share of credit in developing its beauties.

The first name to be mentioned in connection with chrysanthemum history in America is that of Dr. H. P. Walcott, of Cambridge, Mass., who was the first American, either amateur or professional, to raise new seedlings of our favorite flower. His first seedlings were produced in 1879 from seed ripened in his own garden, and were exhibited in Boston in the autumn of that year, at the show of the Massachusetts Horticultural Society, where they attracted but little attention. Dr. Walcott has since that time exhibited more or less every year, and has usually raised about three hundred seedlings each season, many of which have received the highest awards of the exhibition, such as medals and certificates of merit. As Dr. Walcott is not a professional florist, but one of those who engages in this work as a labor of love, he does not make it a matter of business to distribute his novelties, so that they have not become very prominent until the past two years, when Messrs. Pitcher & Manda, of Short Hills, New Jersey, offered them in their special and extensive catalogue of chrysanthemums. Most of these varieties are of decided merit, and have met with the approval they so well deserve. The following is a list of those which Dr. Walcott considers his best :

R. Walcott, Shasta, Savannah, Wenonah, Monadnock, Semiramis, Alaska, Pontiac, Ramona, Nevada, Cambridge, Tacoma.

As will be seen from the names of his seedlings, Dr. Walcott has started a reform in chrysanthemum nomenclature that deserves the attention of all raisers of new varieties. The names should be as short as possible, and such names as Alaska, Shasta and Cortez are preferable to such lengthy appellations as Bronze, Queen of England, Hero of Stokes Newington, or Monsieur le Comte de Faucher de Cariel ; and to have names that can be written on one label, is of itself a great convenience.

The name of Wm. K. Harris, of Philadelphia, also figures prominently among the pioneers of chrysanthemum culture on this side of the Atlantic, and it is safe to say that within the past ten years Mr. Harris has produced more varieties which are now considered standard kinds than all our other growers together. His first seedling of merit, Mrs. Wm. Sheafer, was sent out in 1881, and was awarded a certificate of merit by the Pennsylvania Horticultural Society, and in 1882, he sent out White Dragon, which was awarded a certificate of merit by the Royal Chrysanthemum Society of England in 1886. In 1885, Mr. H. Waterer sent out Puritan, Miss C. Harris, John M. Hughes, Miss Meredith, and Mrs. R. Mason, and in 1886, Wonderful, Robt. Crawford, Mrs. John Wanamaker, Thos. Cartledge, Alfred Warne, Mrs. Anthony Waterer and Lucrece, all of which were produced by Mr. Harris. Each season his productions were increasing, so that in 1887, Mr. Robt. Craig came to the assistance of Mr. Waterer in disseminating the productions of this eminent grower. During that year Mr. Craig sent out L. Canning,

Beauty of Kingsessing, Elkshorn, Mrs. G. W. Coleman,
Mrs. A. Blanc, and Mrs. Wm. Howell, while Mr. Waterer
distributed Wm. Dewar, Public Ledger, Stars and Stripes,
Magnet, Mont Blanc, Colossal, Mrs. Sam Houston and Miss
Anna Hartshorne. Mrs. Joel J. Bailey, which won the fifty
dollar silver cup offered by the Pennsylvania Horticultural So-
ciety, was also sent out this year. In 1888, Mr. Craig sent out
Sunnyside, Mrs. T. C. Price, Mrs. M. J. Thomas, Mrs. John
N. May, W. W. Coles, Mrs. A. C. Burpee and others, while
in this same year, Mr. Waterer distributed Excellent and
Robt. Craig, also from the hands of Mr. Harris, and in 1889,
he sent Mrs. W. K. Harris—which took first prize for best
seedling offered by the Pennsylvania Horticultural Society—
Violet Rose, Ivory, Mrs. Irving Clark, Advance, Mountain of
Snow, Miss Mary Wheeler and others too numerous too allow
individual mention. This year Messrs. Hill & Co., of Richmond,
Ind., sent out of his raising C. A. Reeser, John Lane, Mrs.
Winthrop Sargent, Carry Denny, Reward, Model, Twilight
and White Cap. The colors and tints which were unknown
in this flower a decade ago are now found in all of these varieties. Maroons, crimsons, rose, pink and buff have become
more decided, and with such progress as this in another
decade, the production of a scarlet flower is not to be de-
spaired of by those who have done most in our favored climate
to bring out the newer and formerly unknown shades.

In 1883, Mr. H. Waterer, of Philadelphia, brought an
importation from Japan of some fifty varieties, many of which
were most distinct and beautiful, which gave a new impulse
to hybridizing, as from that time to the present, the new
kinds that have appeared annually are almost numberless.
Among those imported from Japan by Mr. Waterer, we find
the following very excellent sorts : Gloriosum, Mrs. C. H.
Wheeler, Marvel, J. Collins, Duchess, H. Waterer, Pres.
Arthur, Snowstorm, Mrs. Geo. Bullock, Mrs. Vannaman, The

Bride, Hon. John Welsh, Jessica, Mrs. Frank Thomson, and others.

As another successful raiser of chrysanthemums, the name of Mr. T. H. Spaulding, of Orange, N. J., will long hold an important place among the chrysanthemum growers in America. This gentleman sent out his first seedling in 1886, and each year since then many excellent varieties of his production have been placed upon the market. In 1888 he sent out Geo. McClure, Mrs. John Pettit, Cloth of Gold, Eleanor Oakley, E. S. Renwick, Gladys Spaulding, Juno, R. E. Jennings and others. In 1889, George Atkinson, Commotion, Tusaka, Takaki, Mrs. Judge Benedict, We Wa, Brynwood, and many others were produced and disseminated by Mr. Spaulding, and during the present year the new English prize chrysanthemum, Mrs. S. Coleman, and his own seedling, Ada Spaulding, are being distributed. The latter was awarded the National prize in November, 1889, presented by Mrs. President Harrison, at Indianapolis; also a certificate of merit by the Pennsylvania Horticultural Society; first premium by the New Jersey Horticultural Society, and medal of excellence by the American Institute, N. Y. It is a cross between Puritan and Mrs. Wanamaker; of robust habit; a rich deep pink, shading in upper portion to the purest pearl white; globular in shape and neither Japanese nor Chinese in form. Mr. Spaulding is also introducing this year the following varieties of his own growing: Addie Decker, Maria Ward, Garnet, Mrs. Thomas A. Edison, Jas. R. Pitcher, Cyclone, Zenobie, and others.

The following varieties, the first five imported from Japan by Mr. John Thorpe, and the others grown by him, were also first distributed by Mr. Spaulding: G. F. Moseman, Mrs. T. H. Spaulding, Sokoto, Leopard, Mrs. J. N. Gerard; Pauline, Coronet, Dango Zaka, G. P. Rawson and Peculiarity, together with Miss Sue Waldron and Snowdrift, grown by Mr. J. N. Gerard, of Elizabeth, N. J., and Sunset, Mrs. Wm. Barr, Miss

Alice Brown, and Fannie Block, grown by William Barr, of Orange, N. J. There are also many other excellent varieties, either raised or disseminated by Mr. Spaulding, that chrysanthemum lovers now enjoy, several of the seedlings of Messrs. Lord, Allen and Hollis being among them.

There is no commercial house in New England more favorably known to chrysanthemum growers than that of E. Fewkes & Sons, of Newton Highlands, Mass. At one time these gentlemen held the entire stock of Mrs. Alpheus Hardy, and were the first to flower and exhibit it in America ; they still retain the silver medal awarded to its first bloom by the Massachusetts Horticultural Society. It was also from this bloom the first cut was made that illustrated the horticultural papers and catalogues at that time.

The first varieties offered in 1868 by Messrs. Fewkes met with but little sale, and out of their entire collection, we are informed, the variety White Treveana, a small double white flower, was the only one that commanded even a passing attention. The house of Edwin Fewkes & Sons has steadily kept pace with the increasing interest in the chrysanthemum, and to their skill as growers and enterprise as importers we are indebted for the following excellent varieties : Wm. H. Lincoln, Kioto, Neesima, Lilian B. Bird, Mrs. Fottler, Belle Hickey, Emmie Ricker, Nippon Medusa, S. B. Dana, Marian, Clarence, Bryant, Emily Selinger, Flora, Nahanton, H. A. Gane, Jno. Webster, James F. Mann, Lizzie Gannon, Pres. Hyde, and chief of all, the far-famed Mrs. Alpheus Hardy.

The enterprise also of Messrs. Pitcher & Manda, of Short Hills, N. J., has given much to the lovers of chrysanthemums on this continent. In 1889 this firm imported from Japan and distributed the following varieties : Rohallion, Passaic, Kansas, Arizona, Ithaca, Raleigh, Jean Humphreys, and Mrs. Cornelius Vanderbilt. The following of their own production have also been distributed : Bohemia, Indiana, Iona, Iowa, Iroquois, Oneida, Mohawk, Virginia, Pequot, Minnewawa, Connecticut and Mrs. DeWitt Smith. It was this firm also that secured the entire stock of Mrs. Alpheus Hardy from Edwin Fewkes & Son, and first distributed it to the public.

The progress of chrysanthemum growing in America can not well be written without mention of the firm of V. H. Hallock & Son, Queens, Long Island. To these gentlemen we owe the origin of many excellent sorts, to the number of which they are constantly adding, as is evidenced by the list of new varieties that are offered annually to the public through their catalogues. This year (1890) they offer twenty new varieties in one collection for the first time. Among the varieties which they have been instrumental in giving to the public are Mrs. Langtry, W. Falconer, Whirlwind, Pagoda, Sadie Martinot, Frank Wilcox, T. F. Martin, Moonflower, Mrs. Cleveland, F. T. McFadden, Mrs. Potter, Edwin Booth, Prince Kamoutska and V. H. Hallock.

The name of John Thorpe is well known to chrysanthemum lovers throughout America, as well as in England. While associated with Messrs. Hallock & Son, he produced some excellent varieties, and sent out his first seedlings in 1883. He is to-day the leading spirit in the progress of chrysanthemum culture in this country. Since he severed his connection with the firm of Hallock & Son and located at Pearl River, in the same state, he has perhaps given chrysanthemums more attention than at any other period of his life.

Through his instrumentality the National Chrysanthemum Society of America was organized in 1889, a society of which he has the honor of being president. Mr. Thorpe was the producer of that most desirable variety, Mrs. Andrew Carnegie, winner of the Carnegie Silver Cup in New York in 1888, which is one of the best of its color at the present time. It is a matter of the deepest regret to the writer that he has not been able to elicit from Mr. Thorpe more information regarding his seedlings, and other matters of interest in connection with chrysanthemum history in the United States, of which we are sure he has a wealth of information.

While the culture of the chrysanthemum has extended to every state and territory, the work of producing new varieties is confined to a very limited area. Perhaps nowhere in America are more chrysanthemums grown than in the vicinity of Philadelphia, where the climate seems to be particularly well suited to their highest development. The amateurs and professional gardeners around the Quaker City have produced many desirable kinds. Thomas Monahan, a private gardener produced last season an admirable variety, which he named in honor of President Harrison. Thomas Carey, Henry Surman, Wm. Jamieson and James McCleary, all private gardeners, are growers of importance in Philadelphia. W. C. Pyfer, formerly of Lancaster, in the same state, has produced many seedlings of merit, but he is now located in California, where we trust the good work will go on, and be even more successful.

With the exception of a small portion of Indiana, the chrysanthemum raising section of America does not extend over an area of two hundred square miles. A belt of country from Boston, Mass., taking in a portion of New York and New Jersey to Philadelphia, would comprise the nursery from which is disseminated all that is new and beautiful in American seedlings. The west has but little to add in new varieties, excepting some importations of Messrs. Hill & Co., of Richmond, Ind., and a number of seedlings from Messrs. Rieman and Dorner in the same state. What is lacking in the west, however, in the production of new varieties, is amply atoned for by the superior development of the varieties of eastern birth, as is demonstrated at such exhibitions as are held at Chicago, Indianapolis and Cincinnati; and with

such a name as that of John Lane at the front, we may
expect much from the west in the not distant future.   Mr.
Lane is a retired business man,. an enthusiastic amateur in
chrysanthemum culture, and treasurer of the National Chrysanthemum Society.   He has extensive grounds and several
greenhouses, from which his friends and neighbors reap the
benefit, for his flowers are distributed with the most lavish
generosity.   His critical notes on varieties and culture, written in a style wholly his own, always receive great attention.

The chrysanthemum has been exhibited at the shows of the
Massachusetts Horticultural Society in Boston since 1830.
The list varieties exhibited at that time was as follows: Quilled
Flame, Curled Lilac, Tasseled White, Golden Lotus, Large
Lilac, Changeable Buff, Paper White, Crimson, Pink, Lilac,
White, Semi-quilled White, Parks, Small Yellow, Golden
Yellow, Quilled Lilac, and Quilled White, these being exhibited by Robt. L. Emmons of Boston, then recording Secretary of the Society, and Nathaniel Davenport.   The plants
were spoken of as grown in the open ground, and evidence is
given that that the number of varieties at this period was
very small.   They were exhibited on the 20th of November,
and reported in the *New England Farmer* of November 26th,
1830.

CHAPTER III.

Propagation.

THE propagation of the chrysanthemum by *cuttings* is the system adopted in every country in which it is grown. New varieties and the single sorts are produced from seed. Old plants may also be divided to increase the stock, with comparative success, but propagation by cuttings is the method universally adopted, and is by far the most satisfactory. Chrysanthemum cuttings root so freely that few growers give the subject the attention it deserves. In most cases the cuttings are taken with little regard to quality, and planted where they will root most quickly with the least amount of trouble. This method of course may serve the purpose where the finest chrysanthemums are not expected, but in order to obtain the best possible results, strict attention must be paid to every detail of their culture. It is of the first importance that we commence operations with good material, that as perfect a foundation as possible may be laid for future success. There are so many adversities to beset the grower through the long months of culture, that the start should be made under the most favorable circumstances.

It is possible to produce flowers of the finest quality upon plants that are propagated at any time from December to May, but as a rule the cuttings started in February and March give the finest results. When plants are propagated early, as in November and December, there is a long dormant season through which the young plants are compelled to pass, during which the wood becomes hardened to a dangerous degree, and they also require much labor and attention as well as valuable space for at least two months that might be easily avoided. Florists having a plant trade in the southern states, with a demand for strong young plants in January and February, are almost the only class that would get profitable returns from December propagation. With scarce varieties, however, every cutting rooted is a gain, regardless of the season in which the operation is performed, as, if rooted in December, the top may be taken off in March, and the stock in this way further increased, this plan being followed by most florists who desire to produce a large number of plants, or in establishments where quantity is preferred to quality. On the other hand, other matters will be needing attention in March, and there may not be sufficient time to make a judicious selection of varieties, and it is also difficult to obtain shoots in the proper state for cuttings as late as that. By choosing a time between these extremes, as in February, these difficulties are avoided, and the work may be performed with greater satisfaction.

Many growers imagine that in a place suitable for propagation, bottom heat is required, but in reality there is no occasion for it, and those who would be successful should take care that no artificial heat in any form is applied except when absolutely necessary during unusually cold spells. Plants raised in bottom heat rarely produce flowers of fine quality ; while it hastens the process of rooting, the plants are always weak and liable to receive injury where those more hardily reared would remain unharmed. A place where a temperature of forty-five degrees can be maintained, and which is kept rather close, with the cuttings near the glass, is most suitable. If but a limited number are required, the cuttings may be inserted in pots, either singly or otherwise, and placed on a firm, moist surface, such as sand or ashes, but if large quantities are desired an ordinary propagating bed of clean gritty sand must be resorted to, and the same process followed as for rose and carnation propagating, excepting only the heat. Firm and healthy short jointed shoots should be selected for cuttings, from plants in good growing condition. Those of a succulent nature do not make the best cuttings, neither do those that have become hard and woody, and growths that have the appearance of flowering shoots should also be avoided, although they will root and make plants on a pinch.

The cutting should be at least three inches long, and cut horizontally with a sharp knife just below the joint. The leaf at the base may be removed and all the rest retained, if the cuttings are to be inserted singly in small pots. If, however, the cuttings are to be put into an ordinary propagating bed, in addition to the removal of the lower leaf, all the remainder may be trimmed, so that the cuttings can be put close together in the bed and the air circulate more freely through them, and prevent them from damping off. They also have a neater and more systematic appearance in the propagating bed with the foliage judiciously trimmed. When rooted singly in pots, this is not necessary, as the cuttings must of necessity be sufficiently far apart to prevent the leaves touching each other. The small pots that are to receive the cuttings should be filled with a rather fine mixture of equal parts of sand, leaf mold and loam, well drained, with a thin layer of sand on top. With a pointed stick make a hole in the center ; insert the cutting about half its length, and press the soil about it firmly, taking care that the cutting is not bruised or injured during the operation. By this method of propagating singly in pots, the greatest success may be expected, and we would recommend that all specimen and exhibition plants should be rooted in this manner, the extra labor being amply repaid by larger and finer blooms. Where several cuttings are put into a pot, or where rooted in the propagating bed, when the time comes for their separation and potting, the roots must receive some injury, and all checks of this sort must be avoided as far as possible, especially for exhibition plants.

When the desired number of cuttings is potted, water thoroughly and then place in the house or frame prepared for their reception. Here they should be kept close and syringed lightly when dry, until rooted, which will usually be indicated by their putting forth new leaves, when air may be admitted gradually on every favorable occasion, and they will also need more water. When the pots are filled with roots they should be shifted into larger pots in a good compost of finely prepared soil. If the cuttings have been placed in the sand of the propagating house, the skilful grower can tell by their fresh and plump appearance when they are rooted without lifting one from the bed to examine. When rooted in this manner they should be potted in about two and one-half inch pots in a mixture of finely pulverized soil. But as they will soon outgrow these pots, the soil for the first potting seldom receives much attention. When potted, if the weather is bright, they should be shaded for a few days and kept slightly sprinkled until they start into vigorous growth.

In the propagation of the chrysanthemum, the purpose for which the plants are required largely determines which is the best system to follow. All have their advantages and drawbacks alike, so that nearly every grower has his own peculiar method, in which he is particularly successful, and no single method can be universally adopted. The cardinal points, however, are alike everywhere, the minor details alone varying. The wholesale grower who raises his plants by the hundred thousand cannot adopt the system of the millionaire's gardener who raises annually a hundred plants for conservatory decoration, or of the amateur who grows a few dozen for his fall display or city exhibition. The latter can select their cuttings at just the right stage of development and root them according to their fancy, but the wholesale grower simply gets his cuttings when he can, and roots them when most convenient. The weak and the strong, the soft and the hard, all alike go into his propagating bed, where they root and are soon ready for distribution.

Propagations by *division* is adopted chiefly by amateurs who keep their old plants to flower the following season, and is not to be recommended except as a simple means of increasing the stock for ordinary out-door or garden cultivation. It is best performed in March or April, according to the season and the locality in which they are grown. A good time to divide is when the young shoots begin to push out and attain the height of about two inches. The plants should be lifted with a spade, trowel, or old knife, and the process of dissection is easily performed. The old stump should be discarded, and only the young suckers preserved. When possible they should be taken off with the roots attached, as in this case they may be replanted at once where they are intended to bloom, and should the weather be cloudy or moist they will go on and grow without further trouble ; if warm and bright they will need shading for a few days until they show signs of starting into new growth. In dividing the old plants many strong suckers may be broken off without any roots, and these may be treated as directed for ordinary cuttings. The small pieces of rooted suckers are nearly equal to newly propagated plants. This system of division is especially to be recommended for the climate of the South, as there they are hardy and attain a large size, and unless divided annually will become large, unshapely plants, and the blooms be inferior in quality. Never let them go more than one year without dividing. Give them good rich soil, and keep them staked and watered. Keep the ground free from weeds, and hoe occasionally to keep the ground loose. A top dressing or mulching of litter or hay will help them in a dry time.

Grafting is performed in the usual way during the summer months, as young chrysanthemum stems of sufficient substance cannot be had in the winter or early spring months to admit of this practice ; moreover, chrysanthemum wood is of but annual duration, and consequently must be worked upon during the early months of summer in order that the object aimed at may be accomplished before the blooming season in fall begins. These methods are not adopted as a means of increasing the stock, but simply as a means of increasing the number of varieties upon an individual plant, when such a curiosity is desired. Such specimens are objects of admiration in the exhibition hall or conservatory, although it adds no value or beauty to the individual flowers. This is practiced to some extent by the Chinese, and the idea of grafting the more delicate rooting kinds upon stocks of more vigorous growth has sound reason in it for the chrysanthemum as well as other classes of plants, although it is not adopted to any considerable extent.

Inarching is accomplished by tying up the scion plant among the branches of the plant to be used as a stock, the two being grown near enough together to admit of this when in the border. If in pots the contact is secured more conveniently, and as there is no separation between the scion and stock till the union of the two varieties is assured, inarching is often more successful than grafting.

Propagation by *seed*, together with the process of hybridizing, is a branch of chrysanthemum culture to which no hard and fast rule can be applied. Climate and condition must

first be studied, and the operations carried on in the manner
best suited to the circumstances of the grower.   Probably no
two growers adopt the same system, although there are a
considerable number who practice the art with varying success in every country where chrysanthemums are grown.   In
China and Japan the chrysanthemum sheds its seed naturally,
and new varieties spring up as they do among self-sown plants
in this country.   We are not so favored here, as far as we can
learn, although on the sunny slopes of California this condition may perhaps exist.

All seed bearing plants should be grown in pots, small
plants being selected, as they are more easily handled.   Select
the finest bloom and remove the others.   The plants when in
bloom should be kept in a dry airy greenhouse or pit where they
will get plenty of sunlight.   If plants are well established and
somewhat pot-bound they will bear seed more freely.   Select
the finest flower and remove all others, and when in full bloom
clip off the flower leaves with a pair of shears, but not so short
as to touch the stamens or pistils.   The plants to be crossed
should then be kept close together, rather dry, and with plenty
of light and air, thus providing favorable conditions for wind
or insects to assist in pollinating the flowers, as well as for
the use of the camel's-hair brush in artificial pollination.   In
bright sunny weather, where bees and other flower-hunting
insects abound, a good crop of seed may be had by their assistance; but notwithstanding the time and labor required, it is
advisable to pollinate the flowers by hand, using a fine brush,
in the forenoon of bright sunny days.

Mr. T. H. Spaulding, of Orange, N. J., who has been very
successful, describes his methods as follows: "I take the pollen from one bloom on a pointed match or quill of a feather
and place a little in each petal of the flower to be pollinated,
or touch the stamens with it.   This I repeat during several
successive days, at leisure hours.   I think the best plan is to

take a red, yellow, or white, and cross it with another of the same color, but better in constitution or some other quality, rather than to cross indiscriminately.   I also believe that the petals farthest from the centre are likely to produce the best and most double blooms.   After the pollen is set I withhold water, giving only enough to keep the plants alive, and remove them to a dry place to ripen their seed.   When the plant is nearly matured the seed will in most cases ripen, even if cut from the stalk.''

Chrysanthemum seeds germinate freely in from seven to nine days when sown in pots or boxes and placed in a temperature of 60 degrees, and if sown early in spring will produce blooming plants in the fall.   When sufficiently advanced, pot the plants singly in two-and-a-half-inch pots and move to larger pots as their growth demands it.   A six-inch pot is quite large enough to bloom a seedling in the first year.

The treatment of seedling plants differs from the treatment of those from cuttings in that no pinching or care need be exercised as to the shape of the plant.   Mr. Salter used to say that for every chrysanthemum he named and sent out, he destroyed at least two thousand.   This may be discouraging to the amateur, but the truth must be told ; yet sometimes a good variety will appear among a few dozen seedlings that may make the grower's name famous.

The foliage of seedlings is always clean and thrifty and the profusion of blossoms following afford great pleasure to the grower, as no two will be precisely alike.

The chrysanthemum being so freely propagated by cuttings, hybridizing and the growing of seedlings are only necessary when improvement in either size, form or color is sought for. The principal object of the hybridizer should be to improve upon the vigor and color.   Size should not be sought at the expense of these two qualities.   A first-class chrysanthemum should be of free growth, with stiff stems, the foliage clean and clothing the branches up to the flower, while the flower itself should be of good substance, well formed, and of a pleasing color. The colors which are yet to be obtained are a fine clear orange, a clear bright red, and the long sought for blue.

In an interesting letter from Dr. Walcott, of Cambridge, Mass., on the subject of seedlings, he says: "Not one or two years are sufficient to test the claims of a seedling chrys-anthemum for a leading place. When a new chrysanthemum has survived its fifth year it may be regarded as established, and not before, and I am sorry to find that so few stand the test. Jardin des Plantes is still unsurpassed in form and color, and has been for more than thirty years."

CHAPTER IV.

General Culture.

THERE are few plants that will exist under as much neglect as a chrysanthemum, while there are none more capable of being highly developed under suitable conditions than this now popular plant. Out of thousands of amateurs who grow chrysanthemums, comparatively few give them proper treatment. In most cases, after they are set out in spring, a little weeding and perchance a stake to keep them off the ground, is all the cultivation they receive. With such treatment as this one may have a plant in the fall which to most people would appear pretty, but superior flowers or handsome plants can never be obtained in this way. When all conditions are ready to begin planting, select healthy young plants in a fresh growing condition, avoiding those that are rather large and have a hard, woody stem. Such plants were rooted in November and December, were stunted through the winter, and on this account will not make a rapid growth. They are also liable to rust and become unhealthy long before the summer is over. It is far better to secure vigorous plants with soft wood and in a healthy condition. If well rooted they will soon begin to grow with much vigor, and if properly cared for will retain that condition all summer, looking rich and luxuriant when the large woody plants would become stunted.

(50)

After selecting the plants, choose an open spot, where they can have an abundance of sunshine. Make the soil rich to a depth of about eighteen inches with cow manure if the soil is light and sandy. If stiff and clayey, horse droppings may be used, while a little bone dust may be added with good effect: A little sand may also be used to lighten the soil when it is clayey, as the chrysanthemum thrives better in a rich loose soil, and also because they may be lifted in the fall more easily. The plants may be placed out of doors as soon as all danger of severe frost is over; in the latitude of New York, from the middle of April to the end of May will be soon enough, while in the extreme South and all through the Gulf states they may be put out as soon as February, and proportionately later to suit the climates of the intervening states. The time at which they may be planted must be governed by the frost periods in the given locality. The latest season at which they may be planted with success is that which will allow them a sufficiently long period of growth to become well established in the ground before the dry hot days of summer.

Set the plants out carefully, about two-and-a-half or three feet apart, taking care that the roots are moist, and not suffering for want of water. While this amount of room should be given when a border is devoted entirely to them, when grown in a mixed border with other plants a space of two feet at least should be given each individual.

About the first week in June every plant should have the center shoot pinched out—an operation known as "stopping." Care should be taken not to nip it out too low down, only the center bud requiring removal. A strong stick should be placed beside each plant, to which it should be loosely tied. If it is desired to grow the plants to a single stem, all side branches upon the lower part of the stem, and all shoots that come from below the surface of the soil, should be removed as fast as they appear. If, on the other hand, the bush form is desired, all the shoots may be allowed to grow. In a short time there will appear from four to six shoots below the first one pinched out. These must also be stopped when from four to five inches long and the operation continued until the first of August, after which every shoot may be allowed to grow without further pinching back. In stopping the different shoots, always bear in mind the desired future shape of the plant. Loop the different shoots singly up to the main stake, using a separate string for each shoot, not tying them all together like a wheat-sheaf. Later in the season more stakes will be necessary, as the branches will need to spread out so that the air can circulate freely through them and induce their proper development. In putting in the stakes, place them as close to the stem as possible, letting them incline outward. This is done to have the base of the stakes within the earth which will form the ball of the plant when potted, thus avoiding the danger of breaking the plant by removing the stakes during the operation.

At all times during the summer the ground around the plants should be kept clean and well worked, never allowing it to become baked. Water always in dry weather ; chrysanthemums should never be allowed to suffer for want of water. This is best accomplished by making a little basin with soil around the stem of the plant, to prevent the water from running away when poured on, and causing it to soak in directly over the roots, where it will do the most good. A better plan, perhaps, where the supply of water is abundant and many plants grown, is to place them in trenches that can be irrigated at will. Through the intense heat of July and August a little mulch of grass or litter may be thrown over the surface of the ground, close to the stem, to prevent the roots from drying out too rapidly.

The soil for chrysanthemums, when in pots, is a matter which demands considerable attention. To many growers,

particularly among amateurs, the secret of success is supposed to lie in the proper selection of a compost in which to
grow them. This is a mistake, as the best compost that can
be secured.is useless unless the watering and general management afterwards are correct. It is also a mistake to suppose
that soil must be prepared and stacked from six to twelve
months before using.

No absolute rule can be laid down as to what mixture is the
best, as soils differ so much in various parts of the country,
and nearly every grower has his particular compost, made of
ingredients he deems best suited to this purpose, which he
finds in his own particular locality.

Loam, as it is called, is of great importance, and is com-
posed of the top sod or upper surface of an old pasture, cut
below the fibrous roots of the grass. In some places it may
be cut three inches deep, and in others one-and-a-half inches
will be deep enough to obtain all the fibrous parts, as much
depends upon the time the pasture has been laid down. It
should be cut some time previous to using, long enough
for the grass to decay, but preserving the fibrous roots intact.
Such loam should form the staple of the compost, but in some
districts it is hard to obtain. Many growers of chrysanthemums have to content themselves with very inferior soil, and
such growers are very heavily handicapped compared with
those who live in sections where there are large and fertile
pasture lands.

If the sod is light in character and cut where the land is of
a sandy nature, ground oyster shells should be added, but if
the sod is cut from a limestone region, they may be dispensed
with, as the soil already contains too much lime, a large
amount of which is unfavorable to the chrysanthemum, the
foliage through the summer in this case not being of such a
deep green and vigorous character as where the loam is of a
different character. Charcoal is of great assistance in keep-

ing the soil in the pots porous and acting as a storehouse for
ammonia.   If the turf is of a retentive character, the. soil
should be sifted to remove the finer portion, as this prevents
the free passage of water, when it is applied abundantly in
the growing season.   Thus growers having a rather light soil
at their disposal are much more favored than those who have
to depend on soil which is of a clayey nature, as in the latter
the moisture does not escape as readily, and the feeding of
the plants afterward cannot be so frequently and safely carried. out as in the case of light or porous soils.

Manure is the next consideration of importance, and must
be applied in one form or another.   Cow manure is good on
light soils, but can not be approved of for a heavy soil, as it is
far too retentive in character.   The nature of the soil at hand
must determine the quality of manure to be used.   Decom-
posed manure is frequently recommended, but care must be
taken that it is not entirely spent, as such manure has but
little value.   The best manure is that prepared by shaking
out all the straw and reserving little but the droppings, which
should not be used while too fresh, especially if from horses.
When cow manure is dry enough to admit of its being handled
conveniently, it may be used in that state.   Sheep droppings
and the cleanings of the poultry house may also be used
when in this condition.   Bones are also a powerful adjunct in
making up of the compost heaps.   Bones finely ground are
better than when coarse, as the latter do not give up their
manurial properties sufficiently during the short period in
which the plants have to complete their growth.   Dissolved
bones are also beneficial when used in proper quantities.
Soot is a powerful agent when continuously applied, although
when used excessively it has a most injurious effect upon
plants.   Quicklime is useful for the destruction of worms,
which is an important consideration, and the best time to
apply it is when the soil is being prepared for potting, an occa-

sional handful being all that is required. In applying lime it should not be used too freely in soils already charged with it, but for those of a sandy nature no harm will follow in using the quantity advised. Some discretion should be used in regard to sand also, as scarcely any is required if the soil is of a sandy character. Some growers never use sand at all after the cuttings are rooted. If the soil is close and heavy, they add enough of finely broken old lime mortar to make it porous.

When the soil is used for potting plants that have been outside during the summer, one-third manure may be added to the soil ; but in the case of plants that have to be grown continuously in pots all through the summer, much less manure should be used with the soil, as an excess of manure has a tendency to sour the soil, where plants have to remain in it for so long a time. It is best to use a rather poor soil where plants are grown in pots all summer, and feed liberally from the surface by top-dressings and liquid manure. It needs a stiffer and more retentive soil to grow the chrysanthemum in Tennesssee than in Connecticut, so it will be seen that it is difficult to prescribe a single mixture which shall be the best for all climates and soils. We will therefore, suggest a compost for light, and another for heavy soil, which will be found suitable under most conditions in which the chrysanthemum is grown.

For a heavy soil, take three parts of fibrous loam, broken up roughly, taking out the fine soil, one part horse manure, one part decayed leaves, one part of old mortar or lime rubbish, one part of charcoal or wood ashes broken about the size of walnuts, and one-fourth part dissolved bones, and a six-inch flower pot full of soot to every four bushels of the mixture. Where the soil is light in texture, use four parts of loam as fibrous as can be obtained, adding two parts of cow manure, one part of leaf mold, the same quantity of ground oyster shells or mortar rubbish, half a part of dissolved bones and the same quantity of soot as advised for the heavier soil. Thoroughly incorporate the various parts, using all as rough as possible. The action of mixing reduces the parts consid-erably ; therefore if the turfy loam and other ingredients be chopped small at first, the mass becomes too fine by frequent turning. When the collection of plants to be potted is large, and a greater quantity of soil is required, it is well to mix the compost at once for the whole, choosing a fine day, so that the soil may not get wet in mixing. There may be many growers who cannot conveniently procure all the ingredients for these two composts, especially in the case of amateurs who do not wish the trouble of securing the different articles for the sake of the few plants which they cultivate.

We give one more simple but good compost, which nearly all can procure from the material they have at hand, and which will be found to answer admirably under most circumstances. Three parts rotted sod, and one part rotted manure, adding a six-inch pot full of bone dust to each wheelbarrow-full of the mixture. With good care in other respects, this will pro-duce excellent plants. Those who cannot get all the material described need have no fear that they cannot achieve success, for an ordinary soil, with close attention to watering and fre-quent applications of liquid manure, will produce far better results than the most thorough preparation of compost, fol-lowed by neglect of the plant, in their subsequent culture. We have seen equally as fine chrysanthemums grown in the light sandy soil of Connecticut, in the black peaty soil of Illi-nois, and in the red clay of Tennessee.

When cultivated in the ground all summer and taken up and potted in the fall for house or conservatory decoration, the time of transferring them is a critical period, and the pot-ting is most safely done by the middle of August or first of September, if the weather is cloudy and favorable, as it allows the plants to become well established in the pots before the blooming season arrives, while if delayed much later, they will have grown so large that they can not be conveniently potted without injuring the roots or branches. Dry weather is the best time to pot plants from the open ground, as the soil readily drops away from the ball without injuring the roots. Pot firmly and give a thorough soaking at the roots; place them in a shady spot for a few days, keeping the foliage moist by frequent sprinklings, and a few days later they may gradually be inured to the sun, when if any of them still show a tendency to wilt, they may be returned to the shade for a few days longer. After this the pots ought to be sunk in the ground up to the rim, as this keeps them from becoming dry so rapidly; otherwise, when the pots are exposed to the sun, they are more liable to suffer for want of water, and consequently need more care.

Standards, and in fact all large specimens, will need a good top-dressing or thick coat of manure over the surface when the pots become well filled with roots. Cow manure is best for this purpose, as it can be piled an inch above the level of the pot if necessary, leaving a hollow in the center to hold water. They may remain out of doors until there is danger of frost, when they should be moved into a cool room or greenhouse, but not subjected to fire heat, unless needed to protect from frost. The chrysanthemum does not require heat, but only needs protection from the frost, the drenching rain, and the damaging storms that usually occur at the time they are in bloom.

Liquid manure may be given freely after the plants are potted, and have recovered from the effects of the operation. The most successful growers of chrysanthemums attribute no small portion of their success to the judicious application of liquid manure as soon as the plants have filled the pots with roots. The manure in liquid form is most freely assimilated

by the plants, and can be applied at any time desired. It is
best to give it weak at first, and in a short time the plant will
endure and profit by stronger applications of this stimulant.
If the soil is rather dry, always give a soaking of pure water
before the liquid manure is applied. It then becomes equally
diffused through the soil, so that all the roots are fed and none
injured, as might otherwise be the case if watered with strong
manure water while the soil in the pots is in a dry state.

The fortunate grower who has a farm-yard of his own can
have a tank or reservoir for the liquid manure to drain into,
which can then be diluted to suit the condition of the plant.
Where a farm-yard is not at hand, a barrel or cask may be
sunk in the ground and the manure water made for the purpose ; a wheelbarrow full of cow manure, and about a spade
full of soot, the barrel being then filled with water, makes an
excellent mixture for this use. Sheep or hen manure or guano
may also be used with advantage, but guano is dangerous in
the hands of the inexperienced, and when it can be secured
the common barnyard drainings will be safest and most effica-
cious, and will be certain to promote the vigor of the plants
and add size and beauty to the blooms. A soaking of soot-
water once a week will keep worms out of the pots and give
the foliage a rich green hue. Carbonate of ammonia is also a
wonderful stimulant, and used by many chrysanthemum growers ; no other manure having such an immediate and direct
action on the growth of this plant. One ounce to about five
gallons of water makes a suitable solution. Never water with
liquid manure when the plants are dry, but always use clear
water first and then apply the manure. It is best not to apply
the top dressings or liquid manure copiously until the roots
have reached the sides of the pots in which they are to bloom.
There is no hard and fast rule as to the quantity of these
manures and stimulants which should be used. The location,
climatic influences, and the keen observation of the grower,
can alone determine the proportions of each to be used.

As soon as the buds commence to form they must be closely watched. This will usually be about the first week in September, when the grower will have to decide whether few flowers of fine size are desired or a quantity of small ones. We would advise him to select the large blooms, as a few really fine flowers always command attention, where a number of small blooms would pass unnoticed. If the large blooms are determined upon, one-third or more of the blooms must be taken off. This should be done when they are about the size of radish seed, simply rubbing them off with the thumb and finger, carefully preserving the end or terminal bud. It seems a great waste to do this, but having done it once the grower never regrets it. It is best also to cut away all weak shoots, allowing none of them to flower at all, when large blooms are the object in view.

While large plants may be produced by the "planting out" system, it is admitted that where neither labor nor expense are considered, the finest forms, truest colors and best shaped flowers are obtained when the plants are grown continuously in pots, this rule of course applying to a climate where it is necessary to lift and pot them in the fall, in order to bring into the house for final development.

In the climate of the south fine blooms are annually produced by plants that have never been in a pot, and the finest the writer has ever had the privilege of seeing, were grown in the following manner on the grounds of Capt. J. J. Crusman, at Clarksville, in northern Tennessee: A large pit, 102 by 12 feet, was dug about eight feet deep on a slope facing directly south, with a fall of two feet from the back to front wall. This was originally intended to be planted in Marechal Neil roses, but it was determined to grow chrysanthemums in it for the first season. The pit was banked up on all sides and sodded so that nothing but the sash appeared from the outside. The ground also sloped considerably to the east, and a

fall of three feet was obtained in the length of the pit, which
was necessary for drainage.   In the east end, which was completely above ground, was the entrance door.   No artificial
heat of any nature was used.   A three-foot bed was made
through the center of the pit, and one of the same size on
each side, with an eighteen-inch path all around.   The beds
were made by setting oak planks an inch and a-half thick, on
edge all around, the planks being a foot wide, allowing for a
bed of that depth if desired.   The beds were filled about nine
inches deep with a compost of the following proportions : two
thirds sandy loam, one-third rotten cow manure and a six-inch
pot full of bone meal to each wheelbarrow full of this mixture.
The plants were selected from all sources, both new and old,
the foremost object being to get the largest blooming sorts in
cultivation.   About June first the plants, being vigorous and
stocky and in six-inch pots, were planted in the pit, two rows
in the center bed and one on each side bed about eighteen
inches apart, using two hundred and fifty plants in all, and
about two hundred varieties.   The sashes were all left off
until fall, with the exception of every fourth, which was stationary.   Under these stationary sash were planted such sorts
as Mrs. Alpheus Hardy, E. H. Fitler, and others that do not
stand the sun well.   Abundance of water was at hand, and
careful attention was paid to staking, each shoot being tied to
a stake, and not more than four shoots allowed to each plant,
many of the varieties having only two, and some only one,
according to the vigor they showed in making their growth.
About the middle of August a top-dressing of about two inches
was given them of a material similar to that used in the con-
struction of beds, and September first, a top-dressing of one
inch of cow manure, which filled the beds up level with the
edge of the plank, making the soil a foot deep.   The terminal
or crown bud was reserved in most cases, and all other shoots
and buds removed before they attained much size.   By the

middle of October there were flower buds as large as pigeon eggs on many of them, and at this time the sash was put on, chiefly on account of heavy rains, though abundance of ventilation was given daily when the weather was favorable, until the plants were through blooming. Toward the end of October, and early in November, the blooms began to open. The foliage was thoroughly strong and healthy, and the flowers enormous. Each variety was kept plainly labeled, so that visitors could take lists of those which they liked best. This display, in addition to that in another house, 100 by 20, filled with trained specimens in pots, beside thousands of plants in the open ground, was a sight that can be more easily imagined than described. Hundreds of people visited the display daily, and railroads gave special rates from all points, so that for a period of three weeks the display was a common topic of conversation for nearly a hundred miles around, while the number of varieties and the proportions of the blooms were a revelation to all.

When the system of continuous pot culture is followed, the soil becomes filled with roots in July and August, and the plants then require constant attention to watering, as they are at that time making that portion of their growth upon which the flower buds appear. Rain or soft river water is best if obtainable, but if hard or spring water must be used, it will greatly improve by exposure to the sun for some hours in troughs or tubs. When cultivated in pots they require more water than when planted out in a border or square, and it is also essential that they be provided with ample drainage, so that all surplus water may run off quickly, as the plants require a thorough soaking when watered. Little surface sprinklings are productive of more harm than good, as they serve only to induce the roots to come near the surface to get the benefit of them, and with the first neglect of watering, they are destroyed by the hot sun. Nothing but a good soaking, that permeates every particle of soil in the **pot**, can produce the best results.   Syringing the foliage each evening is of great advantage in keeping the plants free from the ravages of insects and in giving the foliage a healthy appearance, ceasing, however, when the plants come into bloom.

Never water a plant that is not dry ; on the other hand, never permit the plant to wilt for want of moisture, as under such conditions a free and vigorous growth cannot be made. When specimens are grown for exhibition, it is best to go over them in the early morning, again at ten o'clock, at noon, and once more after five o'clock, and should the plants be vigorous and growing, at least two of these waterings should be thorough soakings.   As the plants increase in size, and the pots fill with roots, it is necessary to watch the edge of the ball in the pots, as sometimes the soil is pressed out from the pot, leaving a space where the water may trickle down between the soil and the pot, leaving the plants suffering for want of water, although an abundant supply has apparently been given.   A little care given such plants, by pressing down the edges so that the water may not run through so rapidly, will be abundantly repaid by their subsequent vigor.   When the plants are in full bloom, the days will be short and not so warm, so that one thorough watering each day will be sufficient, and in dull weather they may not even require it so often. It is not necessary, at this stage of their culture, to give liquid manure, clear water being sufficient after the buds have developed into blossoms, but care should be taken not to spill it about the floors, so as to cause a moist atmosphere in which the flowers would have a tendency to mould.

A good plan is to water in the forenoon, or at midday, so that plenty of ventilation can be given until the moisture is completely dried away, and the plants will have a pure atmosphere, not overcharged with moisture, in which to pass the night.

CHAPTER V.

Exhibition Plants.

THE rapid strides in chrysanthemum culture at present, when each recurring season outstrips the past, and when exhibitions are being held for the first time in the history of so many communities, evokes from all sides the oft repeated question to the successful exhibitor, "How were these plants grown?" Judging from the interest so widely manifest in the growing of exhibition plants, the subject of the production of finely formed chrysanthemums and splendid flowers is the question foremost in the minds of many in the profession, and of many amateurs that aspire to first honors at their local shows.

The ideal plant in this country and the standard at all our exhibitions is what is popularly known as the bush plant. These are from two-and-a-half to four feet in diameter, of graceful contour, and each branch terminated with a good sized and finely formed flower.

The requirements for chrysanthemum exhibitions differ in various parts of the country. If plants are grown for one of the rural exhibitions, they may be grown in the open ground through the summer, and lifted as the season of flowering approaches, and potted for fall display. These will answer the purpose very well, and the labor of cultivating them will be reduced to a minimum. On the other hand, if the plants are

(63)

to be exhibited in any of the great cities of the north or west, and are to bear the scrutiny of a Thorpe or a Harris before the blue ribbon is attached, a different system must be adopted, and that is, continuous cultivation in pots, as by this method the finest flowers and best results can be obtained.   Cuttings for this, as for other purposes, should be selected from strong healthy plants after they are through flowering, placing each in a two and a-half inch pot, and partially shaded until they begin to root, when the shading should be removed, and the plants kept close to the glass.   In about three or four weeks from the time of potting, the plant will need transplanting into larger pots.   Give sufficient ventilation, that the growth may not become weakly, and keep up a night temperature of 48 degrees, for if it should get any cooler than this, growth would be arrested and a check to the plant ensue.   The plants should always be re-potted as soon as the ball becomes filled with roots, and should never be allowed to become pot bound.   If the cuttings were rooted in February in two and a half-inch pots, the next change will be into four-inch pots, and this will need to be done about the end of March.   If the plants have grown well, the next shift will be into six-inch pots early in May.   It is advisable to place them in the house again for a few days, at least, until root action commences, when, if all danger of frost is over, they may be placed in the open air.

The summer quarters should be a level piece of ground, arranged so that the surface water from summer showers will readily pass away.   Care should be taken not to set the plant in immediate contact with the earth, or worms will find their way into the pots to the injury of the plants.   Some place the pots on boards, and others use slate, but perhaps the best method is to set the plants upon a bed of coal-ashes, thus preventing the entrance of worms, and allowing the water to pass off freely.   In no case should the plants be crowded, but set

far enough apart so that each plant will have sufficient room
for air and sunlight to play about it. When plants are thus
set in the sun and drying winds, it will necessitate frequent
watering on hot days and in windy weather. Gauze or other
shading may be used judiciously, and is certainly beneficial in
midsummer, especially in the climate of the southern states.
It should, however, be removed in cloudy weather, and late
in the afternoon, so that the plants can get the late afternoon
sun and the refreshing dew. If placed on a roller over an
improvised frame work, it could be run on and off very easily.

Shift from six-inch to eight-inch pots, whenever the condition of the roots justifies it, and give the final shift into the pots
in which they are intended to bloom, not later than the first
of August. These should be about ten or twelve inches in
diameter, depending upon the size of the plants. It is best
not to put plants into pots larger than are absolutely necessary, as they look better in pots which are rather small in proportion to their size. Take two plants of equal proportions,
putting one into a ten, and the other into a twelve-inch pot, and
the difference in appearance in favor of the ten-inch pot plant
will be at once apparent.

The stopping of the young growths, and the judicious tying
of them into place, must have close attention. It is better to
tie a little at a time, than to wait until the shoots all get large
and do it all at once. The grower must first fix in his mind
the shape of the plants he desires, and work with a view to
that end, constant attention being the keynote of success.

The last stopping should not occur later than the first of
August, if plants are desired for exhibition before November
10th. When finely formed flowers of good size are desired,
all but the terminal or crown bud should be removed. This
is best performed by using a pointed stick or penknife, but
care must be taken, or rough handling may destroy the work
of months.

It must not be understood that the first flower bud that forms is the one to be retained, as many varieties produce what is known as the summer bud that generally shows itself in May.   When first seen, it usually has three vigorous shoots around it.   This bud is useless and should be removed as soon as it appears ; if allowed to develop, the plants stop growth for a time, and the formation of the next buds will be delayed.   Some varieties, such as Grandiflorum, and others, must not be pinched too late or they will not bloom at all. When the summer bud is removed several shoots will appear below it, and as many may be left as is thought expedient, the variety and strength of the plant alone determining this. Each of these shoots thus formed, will show another bud which is termed the crown bud, and is the one most likely to produce the finest flowers, if it shows itself at the proper time. Occasionally these buds appear in July, and are known as the July buds, but these are too early, and will produce only imperfect or badly shaped flowers.   It is best to remove all buds that appear in July, as by so doing the plants will be induced to make further growth, upon all of which buds will appear about the last week in August or first week in September.   These are the ones to be selected, and the buds that make the finest blooms.   When the buds are selected, all the after growths and small buds that appear in the axils of the leaves should be removed, as they detract from the progress of the selected buds, and could not by any means develop in time to lend any additional charm to the plants during their early blooming period.   If bushy plants are desired, the tender shoots must be carefully tied down before the growth matures sufficiently to make it brittle, when it easily breaks. After all the shoots are carefully tied down, the plants will develop, as they grow, into the form provided for in the first tying down of the branches.   In tying, care must be taken that the loops that hold the branches are not too tight to move with the rapid growth as it progresses. Wire hoops fastened to sticks serve admirably for tying the shoots where a spreading, bushy plant is desired. There must be three or more to each plant to give it a good form. The wire can easily be cut with pliers and slipped out, as it is best to remove it when staged for exhibition. String should be used for the main stem branches, but raffia or matting will do for the laterals. Remove all the large stakes possible at the same time as you do the wire, if plants will be be safe without them, and preserve its shape during the show without their assistance, for nothing can be more unsightly than a forest of sticks in a pot, with only a small branch or lateral tied to each. The center stake, of course, cannot well be dispensed with, but outside of this as few as possible should be used. By commencing early with the tying, as soon as the plants begin to make their growth, a more natural appearance can be given the plant than if much growth is made before the tying operation is commenced. Carefully tie up the laterals about two weeks before they come into bloom. This gives the shoots a chance to turn their buds to the light and assume a more natural appearance when in flower than if just tied down.

Many people raise their voices against this system of tying altogether, as it is unnatural, and although from a truly artistic standpoint the trained specimens may not be all we desire, to follow nature's course would be to leave our choicest blooms to become bedraggled in the mud, and the training and tying become a necessity. It is of course desirable, when art must be brought to our assistance at all, to bring into harmony with nature, adopting the system best adapted to our convenience and the beauty of our plants.

A stout stake in the centre, to which all the shoots are looped up, is about all the training the chrysanthemum receives in England, in many establishments, when grown only for conservatory decoration; but for exhibition purpose the English

even exceed us in the extent of their training. Their standards, half standards, umbrella tops, pyramids and balloon
shaped plants, show that endless care is bestowed upon their
formation. The feeding and watering of the plants will then
be the all-important care. Like human beings they can exist
and flourish on one or more staple foods, but a change of food
occasionally is best, and will produce surprising results. Use
one week a very light dressing of cow manure, old and well
pulverized ; the next, liquid manure, and so on. Soot water
may also be used with advantage at intervals throughout the
whole season.

The care of watering is best entrusted to one man, and if he
is observant, he will soon find out the nature and requirements of the different varieties. Some varieties require much
more water than others, a fact which soon becomes apparent
to one entrusted with their keeping, and he should govern the
supply of water accordingly. If the plants should ever suffer
from want of water and their foliage wilt, it will count against
the final success ; hence the importance of judicious watering.
A good plan is to offer an interest in the final outcome—for
instance, one-fourth the prize—to the man in charge ; it will
wonderfully energize him, and many of the successful growers
attribute much of their success to this plan.

In England, according to custom, the head gardener is the
recipient of all prize money and profits of all kinds, resulting
from the awards made at horticultural exhibitions in favor of
the articles he has exhibited, whether chrysanthemums, orchids,
or the products of the kitchen garden. He carries with him
when he moves, the certificates, cups, medals, and ribbons
that at one time graced some object of his care in the exhibition tent or hall, and proudly shows them as evidences of his
skill.

The standard or tree chrysanthemums at exhibitions, or
wherever seen, always command attention, towering as they

Nymphæa—a Fragrant Chrysanthemum.

do above the bush and trained specimens.   To amateurs, and others not familiar with the growth of chrysanthemums, the standards are all looked upon as plants of several years growth. A massive specimen six feet high, with a finely proportioned head of bloom, appears to the uninitiated as something impossible to produce in a period of ten months.

The plan best suited to this particular mode of culture, and the one usually adopted by the most successful growers, is to take the first strong healthy shoots that spring up after the first of January, cutting them off about three inches long and placing them in pots or sand, as with other cuttings, in a cool propagating house.   In about two weeks they will be rooted, when they are potted into two and a-half inch pots, if rooted in sand, or if propagated in pots, they are shifted into a larger size.   They should be placed in the greenhouse, kept growing without a check of any kind, and repotted from time to time, as each pot in turn becomes filled with roots.   They should be put into large pots at the end of June, and each confined to a single stem until the desired height is reached. They must be kept loosely but securely tied to straight stakes, and no branches, under any circumstances, be allowed to grow.

The height of the standards is a matter of taste or convenience, some preferring to grow them six feet high, while others consider three feet a more desirable height, unless it is desired for some particular purpose.   When this height is reached, the top is pinched out.   In a few days side shoots appear ; these are trained outward, and pinched again and again until the first week of August.   The shoots are so arranged as to form an evenly balanced and well proportioned head, which gives the plant a unique appearance.   No shoots should be allowed to start from the roots or anywhere upon the stem.   Standards should if possible be sheltered from the winds in fall, when their growth is completed, as they are apt

"Single-Flowered" Chrysanthemum.

to be top heavy, and would otherwise perhaps be broken down by the first strong winds of autumn. They are best grown by being kept in pots all the time, since there is danger of losing them when transferring to pots from the ground in the fall, even with the most painstaking care.

In the south, where they are grown as an ordinary decorative plant for the garden, they may be grown and flowered in the open ground with the same attention to training and stopping, as if grown in pots.   If unsuitable varieties are chosen, no amount of care will produce good standards, so that great care must be taken in this particular.

To grow large flowers, the same soil and treatment is required as for the other purposes described.   The plants should not be pinched often, consequently there will not be as many shoots, but they will be taller and less bushy.   Some plants grow eight feet high, others not half that height, according to the variety.   When the very largest flowers are desired, only one flower should be allowed on a shoot, all side shoots being rubbed or pinched out from time to time, and the small flower buds removed.   The terminal bud is the largest and the one usually retained.

Growers for exhibition often confine their plants to one stout stem, every lateral shoot being removed as soon as it appears, and only one bud retained.   By this means of devoting the complete energy of a plant to the development of a single blossom, it is wonderful to what size the blossoms will attain, and where ample room is given and a good supply of plants on hand, the intending exhibitor would do well to follow this method, if he wishes to distance all competitors for large blooms in the November exhibitions.   Throughout the season the plants must be well cared for, and manure water should be constantly applied.   A stout stake should be placed at each shoot, to which it should be securely fastened.   Care in watering and thinning the buds is the chief point in growing large flowers, and with all these points properly attended to, there should be no trouble in securing the finest blooms. The number of shoots allowed to remain on each plant is a matter each grower must determine for himself, being governed by his circumstances and requirements, always remem-

bering, however, that quantity will be at the expense of quality, as the flower-producing capacity of each plant can be
concentrated into one or more shoots, or even into a single
terminal bud. Some growers take out the terminal bud as
soon as it appears, and thin out the lateral shoots to two or
three, and in this manner obtain fine blooms, but not quite
as early as if the terminal buds were retained on each shoot.

CHAPTER VI.

Insects and Diseases.

THE chrysanthemum, like most other things of beauty, is not always free from trouble; like the rose and lily, a number of enemies assail it, but being of a vigorous constitution, it is singularly free from disease, and with some slight assistance its insect enemies can be speedily overcome.

The black fly or aphis is its most persistent pest, and its attacks are chiefly in winter and spring, and if infesting the plants when set out of doors in spring, they are apt to be somewhat troublesome throughout the summer. It is therefore necessary, while the plants are indoors, just before turning them into their summer quarters to thoroughly rid them of all insects that may be upon them, as it is more easily done when the plants are under complete control in the house, than after they are placed outside. While in the house they can all be destroyed by fumigations, or using fresh tobacco stems among the plants on the benches, or on the hot water pipes. The sprinkling of these stems with water at evening just as the house is to be closed up, will cause them to throw off fumes that will prove fatal to the fly, if continued for a few days. If the plants are in the open ground, syringing the infested plants, and dusting liberally with dry snuff or tobacco dust, has a good effect, and is the best means of eradicating the fly.

In tobacco growing sections, where the refuse can be had at a low cost, the plants out of doors can be freely mulched with it a few times during the season, and no trouble will be experienced from the fly. If tobacco is scarce, take a small quantity, place it in a pail or bucket, and pour boiling water on it, and as soon as cool, syringe the infested plants with it, and it will have the desired effect.

The red spider and the mealy bug will sometimes infest the chrysanthemum, but if a water supply and a garden hose are at hand, a thorough syringing every evening will make it unpleasant for them, and they will not seriously trouble the plants. Clear cold water has many virtues, and is essential in keeping the plants clean.

In the fall a brown caterpillar sometimes preys upon the foliage, and there is no remedy for this better than hand picking. Many of our handsomest sorts are also subject to mildew; the Chinese varieties, especially the incurved sorts, seem to be most liable to its attacks. In some seasons the disease is far more prevalent than it is at others.

Black spot, probably another form of mildew, is also a serious evil upon the older leaves. The mildew generally makes its appearance when the plants are housed or sheltered in November. Its origin is attributed by some to cold nights succeeding sunny days, or great extremes of temperature. Overcrowding the plants and insufficient ventilation are fertile causes of mildew, as well as a cold wet soil or bleak situation, leaving outside late in the fall, and dull cloudy weather. Should mildew actually appear, flowers of sulphur dusted liberally on the plant, so as to come in contact with both upper and under sides of the leaves, is the most effectual remedy. The best preventive is to avoid overcrowding in the fall; giving abundance of air through the day, and preserving a dry atmosphere at night.

CHAPTER VII.

Sports and Other Variations.

THE "sports" that are developed from time to time, thus enlarging our collection, are due to the kindly assist- tance of nature. According to Adam Forsythe, the lilac flowers are most likely to sport and frequently change to yellow. It appears that any color is capable of sporting into any other color peculiar to the chrysanthemum. All four varieties of Cedo Nulli have sprung from one. Bronze Jardin des Plantes came from that fine old yellow variety, and Queen of England has sported into six different colors.

Not to discuss their physiological import, the question for the practical man, is, having obtained the sport, how to keep it. In cases of a sport really worth keeping, the first care is to notice how many terminal shoots produced it, for sometimes the new flowers come in a bunch, but more fre- quently they appear singly. Mark the branches and cut the flowers, taking off a few medium sized cuttings from the wood that produced the new flowers, and strike them in a gentle heat. Having done this, cut the plant down, excepting the stem upon which the new flowers were produced, in order to obtain from it during the winter a large number of side shoots for cutting. By this course a good stock of plants will be

"Thousand Sparks."—Shown in Japan.

secured, and in the following season the new flowers may appear; but on the other hand, the old flowers may appear in their stead, and one may discover that so far as raising a new variety is concerned, all his labor is lost. It may happen that the new flowers appeared upon a sucker from the root, in which case the chances for success are greater than when they appear upon bearing wood.

Another excellent plan when a sport is discovered, is to take the plant to a propagating house, turn it out of the pot, first cutting away all the branches except those bearing the sportive flowers, lay it on its side and cover the ball with sand. Spread the branches on the sand of the propagating bed, and cover the entire stem with sand, being careful to have the leaves exposed, as, if covered, they would rot away. Secure the branches firmly, so that nothing can move them about, and hinder the rooting process. Keep all moist, and young shoots will break from every joint. When these are large enough to remove, cut them off and propagate in the usual way. This is better than cutting the stems into lengths to strike, as the hardened wood is slow to root.

As a rule the varieties which originate from sports are self-colored, although there are occasionally exceptions to this rule, and in nine cases out of ten the sport will be at least as good in quality as the parent. But in time sportive characters will develop more colors than one in a flower. There is no end to the range of sportiveness, and it is possible that many varieties will be found that will show peculiarities little dreamed of at present.

Among the inexperienced in chrysanthemum culture, there is much confusion of ideas in regard to sports. Many persons think they are in possession of something new, when in reality they are only bad forms of some variety, caused by allowing the blooms to develop from the wrong bud. There is no necessary correspondence between blooms of a variety that develops its blooms from buds formed at two totally distinct periods, in the growth of the plant.

The question of sports and sporting is an interesting subject, both from a theoretical standpoint as well as in practical study. The general system, so much in vogue, of growing chrysanthemums for large blooms is not favorable to the increase of our varieties by sports, as the side shoots are taken from the plants as fast as they appear, and it is from these side shoots, when they are allowed to grow and develop flowers, that many sports appear. On the other hand, if grown in their natural bush form, sports appear any and everywhere.

Mr. Burbridge, in his excellent work on chrysanthemums, says in regard to sports, that the causes of their appearance are unintelligible to him.

EARLY FLOWERING CHRYSANTHEMUMS seem out of place, when in bloom in mid-summer, and we do not want them so early, for it must be a poor collection of summer flowers that can need the unseasonable help of the chrysanthemum at any time from the first of March to the first of September; but after that date every bloom that can be secured for a period of four or five months seems invaluable. There are numerous varieties that will keep the southern garden or the northern conservatory gay through November and December. There are also some varieties that bloom in January, and most of the medium and late flowering sorts can be induced to bloom later by a system which we shall presently suggest.

It is to the earlier flowering that we now confine our remarks. This class is of great use in adorning northern gardens where late kinds would be destroyed by frosts, filling up the gap between the summer flowers and the November chrysanthemum. They are also invaluable to florists for cut-flower work through October. John Salter was the first to take this class in hand and develop it, as up to his time the early kinds were all of little merit, and calculated to disfigure rather than to adorn a garden. The varieties that were most valued by Mr. Salter for their early blooming qualities, were Precocite, Golden Button, St. Mary, Mad. Pepin and Illustration. Some of these are still in cultivation, but are not of sufficient value to command general admiration. For the last thirty years this class has steadily improved, with the result of a series of beautiful varieties flowering in September and October; so that the introduction of this group is proving more

useful every season, although it must be admitted that there
is still room for much improvement. A pure yellow, a bright
rose, and a full crimson of such a type as Madam Desgrange,
would be of incalculable advantage to chrysanthemum gardens, and no one familiar with the subject would venture to
say we may not hope for such improvements. This section
will doubtless be much developed and add still further form
and color to our gardens during that period when the pot
marigold, calliopsis, rudbeckias, dahlias, sun-flowers and
tritomas appear to be on the wane, and when the golden
rod, hawk-weed, and dandelion look dim by the wayside. The
following is a brief list of available earlier blooming sorts :

WHITE.	PINK OR CARMINE.	YELLOW.	DARK.
Madame Desgrange,	M. Boyer,	Gloriosum,	Roi de Precoces
Madame La Croix,	October Beauty,	M. E. Nicholas,	Sam. Morley,
Pequot,	M. Ghys,	C. Bryan,	Louis Barthere,
Lady Selborne,	Lord Mayor,	Golden Desgrange,	Fleur Parfaite,
Duchess of Fife,	Grace Attick,	Wm. Cobbett,	Capucine.
Elaine.	Martimas.	Golden Shah.	

LATE FLOWERING CHRYSANTHEMUMS.—For the purpose of
prolonging the blooming season of the chrysanthemum, the
late flowering varieties play an important part, especially the
large flowering Japanese varieties that bloom after Christmas.
Special culture and late pinching has much to do with late
flowering, but a selection of varieties best suited to this treatment is of great importance in the production of flowers during the late winter or early spring months, when other flowers
are scarce. To the production of late varieties, as well as the
earlier section, our growers might with profit turn their attention still further, and greatly extend the season of their favorite flowers.

During recent years various cultural practices have been
resorted to for the purpose of obtaining short bushy plants
that would bloom in January and February, which is the most

NIAGARA.—AN ODDITY.

dreary portion of our floral year. The practice generally
adopted to retard them is cut them down to a height of six
inches early in May, when the plants are eighteen inches or
two feet high. This results in a bushy mass of side shoots,

the plants are retarded so that they will bloom later than would otherwise be the case.   A few plants treated in this way from the beginning of May till the end of June will give a fine succession of flowers through January and February.   After cutting back in this manner the plants must be kept moist until the new growth appears.   It must be borne in mind that the practice is not recommended except in the case of decorative plants, as the individual blooms are not as large when so treated.   It is of special value in the production of flowering plants for greenhouse or conservatory decoration.   Late propagation will also induce late blooming qualities, and keeping the plants out of doors as long as possible in the fall is also favorable to this result.

There are some varieties which, under the same treatment as other chrysanthemums, will not bloom until December is well advanced ; such are Late Duchess, Princess Teck, Mrs. Cannell, H. Waterer, and others.   These should be supplied with liquid manure until the buds commence to show color, but on account of the short dull days in which they bloom they will not require as much water during that period as the earlier sorts.   The following is a list of good late flowering chrysanthemums :

WHITE.	PINK.	YELLOW.	DARK.
Pelican,	Hero of Stoke Newing-	Thunberg,	Welcome,
Mrs. C. Carey,	ton,	Gov. of Guernsey,	Mr. Gladstone,
Lucrece,	Mrs. Wanamaker,	Mr. H. Jones.	Bicolor,
Moonlight.	Mrs. F. Thomson,	Goldfinder.	Gloire de Tou-
	Syringa.		louse.

CHAPTER VIII.

Chrysanthemum Shows and Organizations.

THE first chrysanthemum show not of a competitive nature, was probably that held in the gardens of the London Horticultural Society at Cheswick, in the autumn of 1825, when all the recently introduced novelties from China were shown, about seven hundred plants being exhibited. Another was given in 1829, at Norwich; this was by the Norfolk and Norwich Horticultural Society. A show was held in 1831, in Vienna, where, it is interesting to note, more sorts were known at that time than in England. A few years later, in 1836, Birmingham and Swansea, in South Wales, each held shows. After these shows were inaugurated they gained steadily each year in public favor, until every town in England had followed their example, and each successive year's display has outdone its predecessor, until to-day, the craze may be said to be at its height. At one of the recent shows in London, 10,000 people paid for admission the first day, and at Hull, Portsmouth, Kingston, and other places the crowds are surprising. Almost every town in England has a chrysanthemum society, and in all European countries, especially in Belgium and the North of France, the chrysanthemum is becoming a very popular flower, as it also is in New Zealand, Australia and Tasmania.

(83)

It has been customary in those countries to offer valuable prizes for the best grown plants and cut blooms, which has served to greatly stimulate the interest in this popular flower, so that they are now the most attractive of all the flower exhibitions, and thousands annually flock to see them with as much enthusiasm as the Kentuckians exhibit for their state fairs or race meetings.

The Centenary chrysanthemum show was held in Edinburgh, Scotland, in 1889, the receipts at the door amounting to $5,736 in three days. A grand Centenary Festival was held in London in November, 1890, under the auspices of the National Chrysanthemum Society of England.

The people on this side of the Atlantic have now become interested, and chrysanthemum shows have become as popular as in other countries.

Whilst chrysanthemums were shown by the Massachusetts Horticultural Society as early as 1830, it was not until the year 1868 that the first exhibition distinctively styled a chrysanthemum show was held by this society. This was one of the Saturday shows, from twelve o'clock M. to three P. M., and so continuing until 1879, when it was held on Wednesday from twelve o'clock M. to ten P. M. In 1882 it was continued for two days, in 1886, for three days, and so continued until 1889, when it was held four days.

The exhibition in New York in 1882 is the first in that city of which we can find any record. The plants were chiefly from the gardens of Messrs. V. H. Hallock, Son & Thorpe, of Queens, and Wm. C. Wilson, of Astoria. Several following years large shows were held, at which many new varieties were exhibited for the first time. The formation of the New Jersey Floricultural Society, and its annual chrysanthemum exhibit at Orange, has detracted somewhat from the New York shows of late, as most of the plants exhibited in New York came from that vicinity. Their first exhibition was held in Novem-

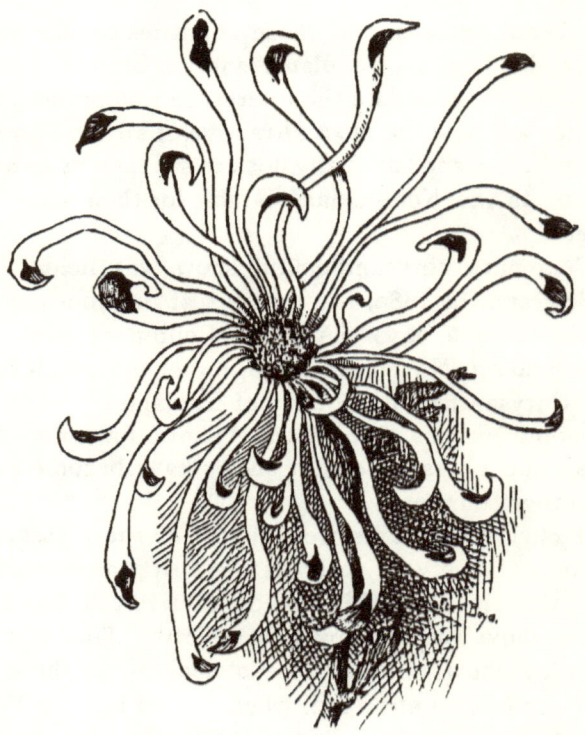

EYE OF THE SERPENT, OR MEDUSA—A JAPANESE FANCY.

ber, 1886, their total receipts being $3,300, leaving the Society a net profit of $2,000 for its three days exhibition.

Since that time chrysanthemum shows have become more general, and once started, they have grown rapidly in public favor, so that their abandonment or retrogradation in a single instance has yet to be chronicled. Philadelphia held its first annual exhibition in 1880, and the shows under the auspices of the Pennsylvania Horticultural Society have now acquired a national reputation. In 1887, Chicago had its first chrysanthemum show, under the auspices of the Chicago Florists' Club. Their second show was in the form of a floral *fete*, upon the grounds of John Lane, in October, 1888, and in the same year also, a display was made in the Eden Musée of that city, in November. Each year since, a most interesting meeting or exhibition has been held, and liberal premiums are annually offered under the able management of the Chicago Florists' Club. Indianapolis, too, had its first show in 1887, and it has increased annually, until now its fame has spread to all countries where the chrysanthemum is grown, and is perhaps the most popular of all the chrysanthemum exhibitions in America at the present time. Cincinnati held its first show in connection with the Exposition in 1888, and in the following year, in Pike's Opera House, a grand exhibition, exclusively of chrysanthemums, was given, and valuable premiums were offered, and have been continued at all subsequent shows. New Haven, Connecticut, held its first display in 1887 ; Montreal, Canada, in 1889 ; Atlanta, Georgia, in 1889 ; Nashville, Tennessee, in 1886 ; Memphis in 1887 ; while the following cities also now hold chrysanthemum shows regularly every fall : Worcester, Springfield, New Bedford and Plymouth, Massachusetts ; Scranton, Germantown, Lancaster and Erie, Pennsylvania ; Hartford, Connecticut ; Camden, New Jersey ; Baltimore, Maryland ; Evansville, Indiana ; Wilmington, Delaware ; Charleston, South Carolina ; Montgomery, Alabama ; Dallas, Texas, and several others.

Every season we read of a dozen or more cities holding their first chrysanthemum show, so that it will probably be but a short time until every city and town of importance will have its annual chrysanthemum show.

While they have been confined chiefly to the large cities of the North and West, we are glad to note that the Southern cities are also falling in line, and the Autumn Queen is given a well appointed reception each season, as she bursts into blossom in the soft sunny days of the "Indian Summer." Nearly all towns of any importance in the South have had for several years a chrysanthemum display, at which no premiums were offered, but an admission fee was charged, usually for benevolent purposes, the plants being contributed from the gardens of amateurs in the vicinity.

Through the enterprise of the Piedmont Exposition Company, of Atlanta, Georgia, the first of a series of chrysanthemum shows was held in the fall of 1890, at which valuable prizes were offered.

The National Chrysanthemum Society of America was organized at Buffalo, New York, in August, 1889, during the meeting of the Society of American Florists in that city. The veteran John Thorpe, of Pearl River, New York, being the moving spirit in the enterprise, took the lead as president, with Edwin Lonsdale, of Philadelphia, as secretary, and John Lane, of Chicago, as treasurer. "If ten years ago it had been said that a National Chrysanthemum Society would be in operation in 1890, many would have said that those who hinted at such a thing would be a good deal safer in some insane asylum, where their utterance would not disturb the minds of their brethren with such absurd predictions." So said Mr. Thorpe soon after the formation of the Society. A year, however, has passed, and the author regrets his inability to chronicle any of its achievements. Probably time is required to lay the foundations of such a glorious institution as we would fain see the National Chrysanthemum Society become. We trust the moving spirits in the organization will pursue the good work so cheerfully undertaken until their fullest ambition is attained, and thereby gain the admiration of all toilers in the world of "mums."

The work proposed by Mr. Thorpe to receive the first attention of the Association is as Follows : *First*, the supervision and discrimination to be given to seedlings before they are distributed ; this is mentioned first because there are so many now foisted upon the market that are worthless, and because of its great importance ; *Second,* the consideration and selection of collections for all purposes; *Third,* the best method of producing the best specimens of all kinds and for all purposes ; *Fourth,* supervision as far as possible over those distributing chrysanthemums, so as to insure their being true to name ; *Fifth,* the formation and establishing of socie-ties in all cities, towns, and villages, where they do not already exist.

A taste for flowers and decorative plants accompanies the development of culture and refinement as naturally as the taste for music or art, and as the florist depends upon this taste for his living, he should endeavor to increase this inter-est by all legitimate means.   In large cities where there are public parks and botanical gardens, well kept and tastefully decorated, the people insensibly acquire an increased taste for fine plants and flowers ; but in communities where no such parks or gardens exist, the grower can best reach cultivated people by a flower show, thus creating an interest in his plants, and developing a market for them.   In the Eastern states as well as in England, flower shows are given because the taste is already cultivated, and the public desires to see the best the gardeners can produce.   The temptation of substan-tial prizes, and still more, the prospect of greater reputation in his community, is an inducement to the grower to make the best efforts possible to surpass his neighbor, so that the combined results of these individual efforts is the display of such a collection as under other circumstances would rarely be brought together.

In most of the large cities where horticultural societies exist, monthly exhibitions are held, at which papers are read of interest to the craft, and subjects of importance in both flori-culture and horticulture are freely discussed.   At the autumn show, however, the chrysanthemum holds chief place.   It has developed so quickly and grandly from its unassuming ancestors that the family likeness has scarcely been retained, and is not easily recognized except by those who have an intimate acquaintance with the plants. Both Chinese and Japanese types have produced so many different individuals of marvelous beauty, that at present they are named by the hundreds, thousands perhaps appearing every year to displace their less favored predecessors. So great has been the demand for new varieties, that one dollar is considered a fair price for the merest twig that the florist must cultivate for nearly a year before he can see it bloom. If it were not for the fostering influence of the shows this spirit would soon weaken and die.

One who has ever seen a chrysanthemum show will need no further invitation to following exhibitions, than the simple announcement of time and place. Those who have never seen a chrysanthemum show should by all means avail themselves of the first opportunity that presents itself, and they will never regret it. When going to the show, above all do not forget the children ; they have a natural love for flowers, and nothing can give them more lasting pleasure and happiness, than the cultivation of this love of theirs, until they and the flowers are fast and inseparable companions.

NOTES ON EXHIBITIONS.—Numerous innovations are urged in the way of exhibiting chrysanthemums, and it is well to encourage all practical ideas and add new features. We might borrow from the French the method of grouping and displaying plants in bloom, the prize to be awarded for novelty, combined with good taste. All effort to "dress" or rather to deform the bloom should be discountenanced. This practice, however, has happily never been indulged in to a great extent on this side of the Atlantic. To one possessing a sense of propriety and good taste, what is more ridiculous than to exhibit the blooms on flat cards or boards, squeezing them out to their fullest extent ; to curl their petals with ivory tongs, and snip and contort them with tweezers, as well as to insert foreign petals that deprive them of all their grace and beauty !

·There is an instance on record where an enterprising competitor, by a cunning trick, secured for several years the premium for the finest cut flowers at the Liverpool Chrysanthemum Show.   The blooms of the Chinese varieties were most shown in those days ;   they were exhibited on a light wooden bench sloping to the front like a writing desk, with numerous holes in its top through which the stem was passed to the inside, where a zinc tube was usually fixed which contained water to receive the end of the stem.   By this means the blooms, in many cases, especially the flat spreading sorts, were drawn tightly down on the board, or exhibition stands, as they were called.   This mode of exhibition afforded ample facilities for the would-be prize winner, so that in performing the operation of "dressing" his blooms he brought his cunning into play.   With the aid of tweezers and glue pot, several blooms were used to make one, by taking the finest petals from choice flowers, thus greatly augmenting the size of the exhibition blooms that he was so long famous for growing(?).   So dexterously did he unite the parts that he succeeded in baffling both his competitors and the judges for years.   The exhibitor who could successfully employ such a device at one of our exhibitions, where the blooms are exhibited in vases or tall glasses, would indeed be a genius !

The schedules of shows should be drawn up by people of refined tastes.   Beauty of petal, form and color, are more to be sought than monstrosities that rival in form the Globe artichokes.   Prizes might also be offered for single chrysanthemums.   Intending exhibitors should be careful that they thoroughly understand the meaning of the schedules or regulations of the society offering prizes.   If the slightest doubt is felt, a clear idea of what is meant should be obtained from the

HARRY T. WIDENER.

secretary of the exhibition, or disappointment may result on account of exhibiting in the wrong class; being disqualified for showing clusters of flowers when individual blooms were expected, or showing bush plants, when plants grown to a single stem were to be exhibited. Be sure that everything is distinctively understood, and if plants or flowers must be sent a considerable distance, make such calculations that they may arrive at the time designated by the promoters of the exhibition.

In the transportation of specimen plants, the stakes should be drawn together by means of a stout string, as they travel more safely and are less liable to be broken when tied in this manner. As soon as the plants reach the exhibition hall, the stakes may be pressed back to their original position, which they will retain by pressing the dirt firmly around the base of each.

The shipping of cut flowers to exhibition points is always attended with anxiety, and to have them arrive in perfect condition requires great care. Those having boxes made expressly for the purpose do not require any suggestions, but the amateur who has no complete outfit will do well to observe the following hints : All flowers should be cut and placed in water at least twenty-four hours before shipping. Flowers that are opening too early should be cut at once, with long stems, even if a week before the time, and placed in a cool dark shed or cellar, where the atmosphere is dry. A piece of the stem should be cut off every third day, and the water changed.

In packing, wrap each flower carefully in tissue paper, just tightly enough not to bruise. They should then be placed in boxes or baskets, in tiers, so that they may not press upon each other. In boxes, strips should be nailed far enough apart to prevent the flowers from chafing, the stems to be held in place with other strips, using damp paper as a packing between each layer of stems. The same method should be carried out in basket packing, except that strong string is to be used instead of wooden strips.   Do not allow the petals to become wet during packing.   In staging the flowers, all those with long and drooping petals will require to be gently shaken before placing in position, remembering always to make a new surface at the end of each stem by cutting off a piece before again placing them in water upon the stage. Labeling should be legibly and neatly done, placing the names conveniently in front of each flower.   In arranging the flowers, the large ones should be at the back, the smaller ones forming the front rows.

CHAPTER IX.

Classification.

EVERY chrysanthemum grower is well aware that the large flowering varieties have for many years past been divided into certain well marked distinctive sections, and that more recently they have been classified under the heading of Incurved, Reflexed, Anemone, Japanese, Japanese Reflexed, and Japanese Anemone. The first attempt to classify the chrysanthemum was by Haworth, in 1833, at which time there were included only forty-eight varieties, which were divided into six sections as follows:

Ranuculus-flowered,	Marigold-flowered,
Ranuculus-flowered, incurved,	Tassel-flowered,
China-Aster-flowered.	Tassel-flowered, double.

In 1836 another writer contributed a new arrangement or classification of the chrysanthemum, the basis of which was to group varieties in classes of the same color. Twelve divisions are given, and it appears to be of value only from the fact of its containing a table of fifty-nine sorts, which were all those in cultivation at the close of the preceding year.

The classification of the chrysanthemum at the present day is a matter of no small difficulty. The hybridizers have worked much improvement in the different classes, owing to

(94)

FABIAU DE MEDIANA.

the freedom with which they respond to their numerous experiments.   The different classes have been so crossed and intermixed that many of them have lost their identity.   Several varieties at the present time are of doubtful classification ; even the good old Cullingfordii, so long known as a prominent type of the true reflexed section, came near being tossed into a new class by the National Chrysanthemum Society of England.

JAPANESE.

A positive definition cannot be given to embrace all the numerous varieties that claim relationship to this class at the present time.   The greater numbers of leading varieties are so distinctly marked that almost each variety would require a special description, although the general range of character can be indicated without regard to colors, which are much more diversified, brighter and richer than in any other class. The forms of the florets and blooms are ample for distinguishing the chief types.   In all well developed Japanese blooms the short tubular disk florets are absent, their place being taken by florets either flat, fluted, quilled or tubulated ; of varying length, from short straight spreading florets, to long drooping, twisted or irregularly incurved ones.   In breadth the petals also vary much, some being an inch in width, while others are scarcely larger than a stout thread ; some also have the tip of the florets cupped, hollowed or curved upwards, or they are strangely lacerated.   The great variety of characters has led to the proposal of several different methods of classification, founded upon the form of the florets.   One makes three groups : first, ribbon florets, like Meg Merrilies ; second, twisted, as Yellow Dragon ; third, thread, like Cossack. Another makes four sections ; flat florets, like Peter the Great ; florets partly quilled, like Soliel Levant ; florets fluted, like Cry Kang, and florets incurved, like Comte de Germiny. It is not our purpose here to attempt to divide the main group up into these separate classes. Following the catalogue of the National Society of England, we separate but one section from the main group, namely the Japanese Reflexed, all of which, however, can be exhibited in the ordinary Japanese class.

Japanese Types.

Avalanche,	L. Canning,	Mad. Baco,	Etoile de Lyon,
W. W. Coles,	Mrs. W. A. Harris,	Eynsford White,	Mrs. Irving Clark.

Japanese Incurved Types.

Ada Spaulding,	Grandiflorum,	Edwin Molyneux,	Thunberg,
Comte de Germiny,	Pelican,	Stanstead White,	Mr. H. Cannell.

JAPANESE REFLEXED.

The institution of this group may be regarded as an experiment, and it is possible that some slight modification may be requisite when it is thoroughly tested. The accepted type for this section is Elaine, with flat, straight, spreading or reflexed florets; and a number of varieties, with both large and small blooms, can be selected, in which these characters are sufficiently well marked to render grouping an easy matter.

Japanese Reflexed Types.

Alcyon,	Phœbus,	Vallee d' Andorre,	Jeanne Delaux,
Elaine,	Pres. Hyde,	La Triumphante,	Mad. C. Desgranges

INCURVED.

The varieties belonging to this section are chiefly of Chinese origin. They are distinguished by the globular form and regular outline of the flowers. The incurved flower should be as nearly the shape of a globe as possible, the florets broad and smooth, regularly arranged, round at the tip, and the color clear and decided. A hollow center or a prominent eye is a serious defect, as is also a roughness in the flowers or unevenness in outline and want of freshness in the outward florets. The entire class is characterized by an excellent habit of growth and is good for specimens.   As the name implies, all the florets, which are strap-shaped, curve towards the center, and only the backs of the florets are seen in the most perfect flowers.

Incurved Types.

Empress of India,	Jardin des Plantes,	Mrs. S. Coleman,	Violet Tomlin,
Queen of England,	Mrs. Heale,	J.anne d' Arc,	Golden Beverly.

REFLEXED.

The Reflexed varieties differ chiefly from the incurved by the outward or reflex curve of the floret, so that it is chiefly the inner surface of the floret which is seen.   The varieties forming this class are vigorous yet compact growers.   The flowers are of medium size, more or less spherical in form, and are remarkable for their bright and effective colors.   The flowers should be perfectly circular in outline, without a trace of thinness in the center, and with broad overlapping florets.   The flowers of most of the reflexed varieties are too flat, but are valuable for their distinct character and rich coloring, while the greater proportion of them make good specimens.

Reflexed Types.

Cullingfordi,	Julia Lagravere,	White Christine,	Phidias,
Annie Salter,	Dr. Sharp,	Webb's Queen,	Temple of Solomon.

LARGE ANEMONES.

"The distinctive characteristic of the flowers of this class is their large size, high, neatly formed centers and regularly shaped ray florets.   The Large Anemones have two distinct kinds of florets, one the quill, forming the center or disc ; and the other flat and more or less horizontally arranged, forming the border or ray florets.   In the flowers which most nearly approach perfection, we have broad ray florets, so regularly arranged as to form a circle, and the center hemispherical, with no trace of hollowness."

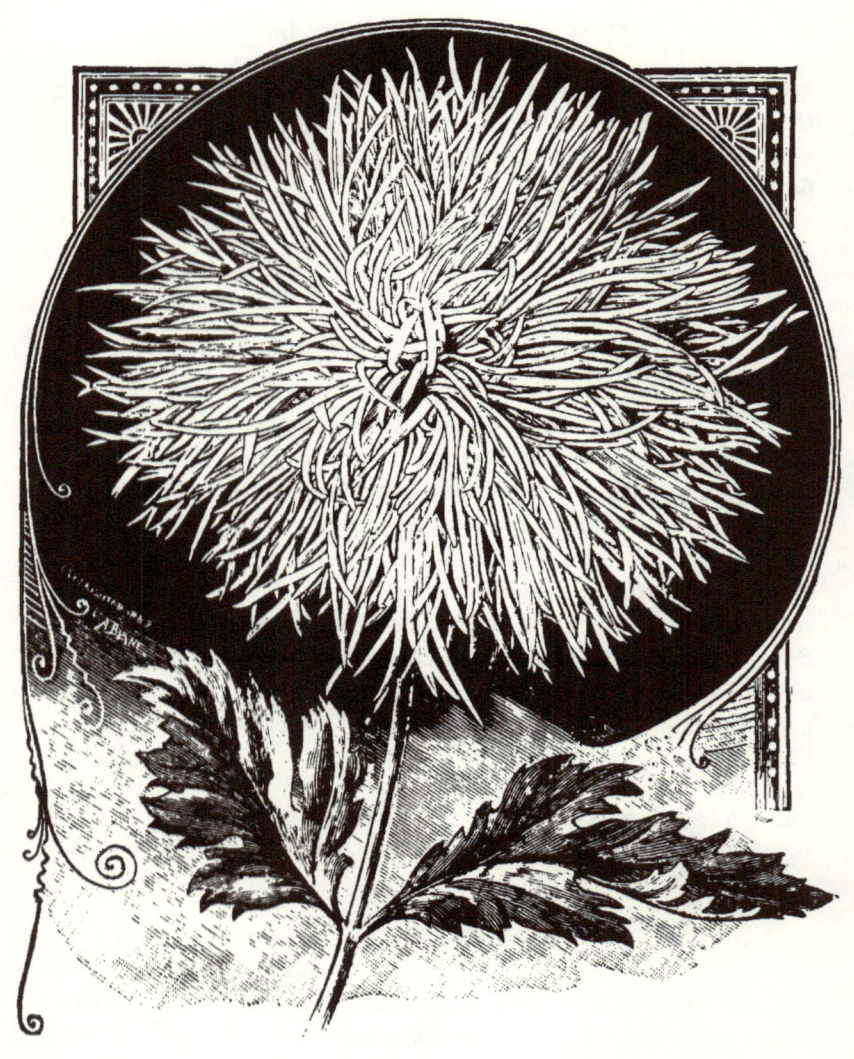

One of the New Japanese forms.

Large Anemone Types.

| Thorpe, Jr., | Geo. Sand, | Gladys Spaulding, | Gluck, |
| Louis Bonamy, | Mrs. M. Russell, | Mrs. Pethers, | Aquisition. |

JAPANESE ANEMONES.

"The flowers of the varieties constituting this group are remarkable for their large size and fantastic form. The disc is more or less regular in form, but the ray florets vary considerably in length, breadth and arrangement ; in some flowers they are narrow and much twisted, in others they are broad and curled, and in some instances the ray florets droop and form an elegant fringe."

Japanese Anemone Types.

| Fabian de Mediana, | Mad. R. Owen, | Sabine, | Ratapoil. |
| Sœur Dorothee Souille, | Duchess of Edinburg, | Mad. Berthe Pigny, | Bacchus. |

POMPONS.

These are all small compact blooms, and are favorites with many on account of their neat growing habit and free blooming qualities. The French growers gave them this name from the resemblance of the flower to the tuft or pompon upon the soldiers' caps. The blooms are nearly globular, being slightly flattened and average about one-and-a-half inches in diameter, the florets of each bloom being of a single kind.

Pompon Types.

| Bob, | General Canrobert, | Snowdrop, | Souvenir de Jersey, |
| Cedo Nulli, | President, | Osiris, | Val d'Or. |

POMPON ANEMONES.

"The Anemone Pompons are of a dwarf growth, having small flowers, with a center or disc of quilled florets, and more or less regularly arranged ray florets. As in the large anemones, the disc should be high, full and neat, and the ray florets flat, and so regularly arranged as to be more or less circular in outline."

Pompon Anemone Types.

| Queen of Anemones, | Virginale, | Marguerite de Coi, | Sydonie, |
| Mr. Astie, | Rose Marguerite, | Miss Nightingale, | Calliope. |

SWEET SCENTED CHRYSANTHEMUMS.

There have been several varieties in cultivation possessing a noticeable perfume, but it was not until the introduction of that delicately perfumed variety, Nymphæa, two seasons ago, that they became generally known, and claimed attention on account of their fragrance. This variety is of American origin ; the flowers are of the purest white, and about two inches in diameter. They have somewhat of the form and fragrance of the well known pond lily, being borne separately on long stems. They are extremely valuable for cut flowers, while their delicate perfume and chaste character make them desirable for the finest floral work. The variety is of vigorous growth and make fine specimen plants. The following varieties are sweet scented :

| Nymphæa, (see cut, p. 69), | General Canrobert, | Progne, |
| Scapin, | Dr. Sharp, | Lord Derby. |

SYNONYMS.

The subject of double named or synonymous chrysanthemums is a matter of no small importance to the cultivator, and is a practice that cannot be too strongly condemned. This practice is followed mainly for the purpose of enhancing their value from a commercial point of view, although it may sometimes have arisen from accident ; but in either case the disappointment caused is alike. In order to mitigate as far as possible the annoyance likely to arise from two or more names being given to one variety, we publish a list of those most likely to be met with at the present time, which is based upon a list published by N. Davis, of Camberwell, England, supplemented by additions from other sources.

CHRYSANTHEMUM SYNONYMS.

Name.	Synonym.
Alice Bird	Buttercup.
Alix	Voltaire.
Ambrosia	Harry Townsend.
Angelina	President Sanderson.
Albert de Norios	Albert.
Aigle d'Or	Berrol, Drin Drin.
Album Striatum	Striatum.
Alderley	Mrs. Huffington.
Aregina	Inner Temple.
Beethoven	St. Patrick.
Boule de Argent	Silver Ball.
Baron Beust	Bernard Palissy.
Beauty of St. John's Wood	Princess of Wales.
Beaute du Nord	Bixio.
Bendigo	Mabel Ward.
Belle Paule	Belle Pauline.
Bertier Rendatler	Mme. Bertier Rendatler, Curiosity.
Bob	Maroon Model.
Bonnington	Fernand Feral.
Bouquet Fait	M. Planchenau.
Bruce Findlay	Golden Empress of India, Lord Alcester.
Belle Hickey	Empress of Japan.
Chinaman	La Chinoise.
Christin, (White)	Mrs. Forsyth.
Canary Cherub	Canary.
Comte de Morny	Purple Pompon.
Christmas Number	Princess of Teck.
Carmen	Carmien.
Ceres	White Ceres.
Cossack	The Cossack.
Claire Alonzio	Golden Mad. Domage.
Chromatelle	Gloire d'Or.
Charlie Sharman	W. M. Singerly.
Christmas Eve	Mrs. H. Cannell.
Crystal Wave	Stonewall Jackson, Mrs. Potter.
Defiance	Marguerite de Coi.
Delice d'Automne	Rose Mignon.

LEOPARD

Name.	*Synonym.*
Delphine Caboche	Miquellon.
Dr. Bois Duval	Scarlet Gem, Little Bob.
Dr. Rozas	Dr. Rogers, Dr. Rossa.
Drin Drin	Berrol.
Elaine	Mrs. Marsham, White Aigle.

Name.	*Synonym.*
Elsie	Eliza.
Emperor of China	Webb's Queen.
E. C. Jukes	Monsieur Devielle.
Early Rose Queen	La Frisure.
Empress of India	Lady St. Clair, Snowball, White Queen, Mrs. Cunningham.
Erectum Superbum..	The Daimio.
Early Red Dragon	L'lle des Plaisirs.
Emily Dale	Golden Queen of England.
E. Sanderson	Mr. Evans.
Empress of Japan	Belle Hickey.
Flamme du Punch	Punch.
Fleur de Marie	George Hock, Mr. Cole.
Fabias de Maderanaz	Fabian de Mediana.
F. A. Davis	Jeanne Delaux.
Favorite de Solleville	Marguerite Solleville.
Fernand Feral	Bonnington.
Flora	Yellow Perfection, Late Flora.
Franconette Dufour	Mad. Franconette Dufour.
Gillardia..	Val d'Andorre.
Golden Empress of India	Bruce Findlay.
Gloire de France	La France.
Golden Eagle	Orange Perfection.
Golden Circle	Golden St. Thais.
Golden George Glenny	Mrs. C. H. Glover, Mrs. Dixon.
Golden M'lle Marthe	Miss Oubridge.
Golden Queen of England	Emily Dale.
George Gordon	L'Africaine.
Geo. Hock	Fleur de Marie.
Gloire d'Or	Chromatelle.
Glory	Sarnia Glory.
Golden Dragon	Yellow Dragon.
Golden Jardin des Plantes	Golden Mad. Domage.
Golden Mad. Castex Desgrange....	G. Wermig.
Golden Mad. Domage	Golden Jardin des Plantes.
Golden Rhine	L'Or du Rhin.
Grandiflorum	Mr. Barnes.
Gloire Rayonnante	Porcupine, Hedgehog.
Gold	Mrs. R. Elliott.
Harry Townsend	Amy Furz.

Name.	Synonym.
Helvetie	Helvetia.
Hebden Bridge	Berrol.
Illustration	Lucinda.
Incognito	Mrs. Sharp.
Inner Temple	Aregina, Refulgence.
Jeanne Delaux	Japon Fleuri, F. A. Davis.
Jardin des Plantes	Mad. Domage.
John Salter	Mrs. Howe.
J. Hillier	La Bienvenue.
Jeanne D'Arc	Mad. Madelein Tezier.
Khedive	The Khedive.
Lord Derby	Odoratum Purpureum.
Lord Alcester	Princess Imperial.
L'Africaine	George Gordon.
L'Aube Matinale	L'Aube Nationale, Salmoneum plenum.
L'Infante d'Espagne	Soliel Levant.
L'Or du Rhin	Golden Rhine.
La Bienvenue	J. Hillier.
La France	Gloire de France.
La Frisure	Early Rose Queen.
Lady St. Clair	Empress of India.
Lady Trevor Lawrence	Mrs. Beale.
Late Duchess	Virginale.
Late Flora	Flora.
La Chinoise	Chinaman.
Little Bob	Scarlet Gem.
Lucinda	Illustration.
Luxembourg	Mrs. Wood.
Lakme	Lincoln's Inn.
Lincoln's Inn	Lakme.
Mrs. Marsham	Elaine.
Mrs. George Rundle	Mrs. George Parne.
Mrs. Sharpe	Incognito.
Mrs. Wood	Luxembourg.
Mrs. George Parnell	Mrs. George Rundle.
Mrs. Frank Thomson	G. W. Drover.
Mottled Beverly	Rotundiflora.
Mount Edgcumbe	Mrs. George Rundle.
Mr. Piercy	Mad. Pecoul.
Mrs. Cunningham	Empress of India.

Name.	Synonym.
Mrs. Huffington	Alderley.
Mrs. R. Elliott	Gold.
Mrs. Irving Clark	Volunteer.
Mrs. J. N. Gerard	Mrs. Dunnet
Mrs. Dunnett	Mrs. J. N. Gerard.
Marvel	Mrs. H. Wellam.
Mrs. H. Wellam	Marvel.
Mrs. H. Cannell	Christmas eve.
Mrs. Potter	Stonewall Jackson.
M. Castex	Nouvelle Alveole.
Mrs. Alpheus Hardy	Ostrich Plume.
Mabel Ward	Bendigo.
Mme. Bertier Rendatler	Bertier Rendatler.
Mme. Desgranges	G. Wermig.
Mad. Domage	Jardin des Plantes.
Mme. Greame	Virginale.
Mme. Pilbetz	Leopold Catalin.
Mme. Seux	Mme. Seny.
Mlle. Augustine Gauthent	Augustine.
Madeleine Tezier	M'lle Madeleine Tezie.
Marguerite de Coi	Defiance.
Marguerite de York	Sunflower.
Marguerite Solleville	Marquis de Telleville.
Marie Longarre	Illustration.
Maroon Model	Bob.
Martha Harding	Thomas Todman.
Miquellon	Delphine Cabcche.
Miss Marechaux	Miss Thurza.
Miss Oubridge	Golden M'lle. Marthe.
Miss Thurza	Miss Marechaux.
M. Deveille	E. C. Jukes.
Mr. Dixon	Mrs. Dixon.
Mr. J. J. Hillier	Mr. John Laing.
Mr. John Laing	Mr. J. J. Hillier.
Mr. Mancy	Petite Mignon, M. Dufoy.
M. Moussillac	Mousillac.
M. Planchenau	Bouquet Fait.
Mr. Barnes	Grandiflora.
Mr. Corbay	Mr. Drain.
Mr. Cole	Fleur de Marie

MISS ALPHEUS HARDY.
Showing a well-grown Pot Plant.

Name.	Synonym.
Mr. Evans	Oliver Cromwell.
Mrs. Howe	John Salter.
Mr. J. Starling	Tricolor.
Mr. Murray	President.
Mrs. Beale	Lady Trevor Lawrence.
Mrs. C. H. Glover	Golden George Glenny.

Name.	Synonym.
Mrs. Mary Morgan	Pink Perfection.
Mrs. Forsyth	White Christine.
Mrs. Dixon	Golden George Glenny.
Mrs. H. J. Jones	Yellow Ethel.
Nanum	Sistou.
Nouvelle Alveole	M. Castex.
October Beauty	M. E. Nichols.
Oliver Cromwell	Mr. Evans.
Orange Perfection	Golden Eagle.
Princess Imperial	Lord Alcester.
Princess of Teck	Christmas Number.
Princess of Wales	Beauty of St. John's Wood.
Pink Perfection	Mrs. Mary Morgan.
President Sanderson	Angelina.
Peter the Great	The Czar.
Pollion	Saddington, St. Crouts.
Pompone Toulousaine	Perpetual Toulousaine.
President	Mr. Murray.
Punch	Flamme du Punch.
Purple Pompon	Comte de Morny.
Perpetual Toulousaine	Pompone Toulousaine.
Porcupine	Gloire Rayonnante.
Primrose League	Yellow Snowdrop.
Queen of England	Blush Queen of England.
Quintus Curtius	Curtius Quintus.
Refulgence	Inner Temple.
Rose Mignon	Delice d'Automne.
R. Ballantyne	Source Japonaise.
Rotundiflora	Mottled Beverly.
Ralph Brocklebank	Mr. Ralph Brocklebank.
Roseum Superbum	Souvenir de Haarlem.
Robert Bottomley	Lady Lawrence.
Salmoneum plenum	L'Aube Matinale.
Scarlet Gem	Little Bob.
Silver Ball	Boule de Argent.
Sistou	Nanum.
Snowball	Empress of India.
Soliel Levant	L'Infant d'Espagne.
Source Japonaise	R. Ballantyne.
Souvenir de Amsterdam	Amsterdam.

Name.	Synonym.
Souvenir de Haarlem	Roseum Superbum.
Striatum	Album Striatum.
St. Mary	Souvenir d'un Ami.
Sultana	Ville d'Hyeres.
Sunflower	Marguerite de York.
St. Crouts	Saddington.
St. Patrick	Beethoven.
Sarnia Glory	Glory.
Stonewall Jackson	Mrs. Potter, Crystal Wave.
The Daimio	Erectum Superbum.
The Globe	White Globe.
Thomas Tedman	Martha Harding.
Thorpe Junior	J. Thorpe, Jr.
Tricolor	Mr. J. Starling.
The Czar	Peter the Great.
Thurza	Miss Marechaux.
Undine	Little Beauty.
Val d'Andorre	Gillardia.
Ville D'Hyeres	Sultana.
Virginale	Late Duchess.
Volunteer	Mrs. Irving Clark.
Webb's Queen	Emperor of China.
White Aigle	Elaine.
White Beverly	Beverly.
White Queen of England	Empress of India, Snowball.
William Holmes	Mr. William Holmes.
White Christine	Mrs. Forsyth.
White Queen	Empress of India.
White Saddington	White St. Crouts.
White St. Crouts	White Saddington.
W. M. Singerly	Charlie Sharman.
Yellow Dragon	Golden Dragon.
Yellow Ethel	Mrs. H. J. Jones.
Yellow Snowdrop	Primrose League.

CHAPTER X.

Select Lists of Varieties for Various Purposes.

THE wonderful progress made within the past few years in the culture of the chrysanthemum renders it difficult to give a list of varieties suitable for each particular style of culture that would be acceptable to all growers. Nearly every grower has his favorites for each special system of cultivation. Within the past few years new kinds are annually introduced that eclipse many of the favorites of each preceding year. To an American grower of the present day it is a little amusing to look over a few of the works by English and other writers and see the varieties there enumerated as the finest in their respective classes. With some exceptions there is not one of them that would pass muster among the great army of home-raised seedlings that annually come into our plant commerce. Many of those varieties that occupied a prominent position in their respective classes, but a few years since, are now relegated to obscurity, and varieties of more recent introduction occupy well nigh all the honored positions. In view of this it is with hesitation we give a list of the best varieties at the present time, lest future chroniclers might deride us for our choice of to-day. However, if the next decade will produce varieties as superior to these of the present time, as the varieties of recent introduction are to those grown ten years ago, we will be so thoroughly elated at the triumph as to take with complacency any derision of our suggestions.

The following lists are selected with much care, and will be found most suitable for the purpose named.   We omit varieties of this year's introduction :

Forty-eight of the best varieties for specimen plants or garden decoration.

Name.	Color.
Cullingfordii	Red.
Mad. C. Audiguier	Pink.
Mrs. Frank Thomson	Pink.
Domination	White.
Duchess	Red.
Ada Spaulding	Pink.
Lord Byron	Bronze.
Mrs. Bullock	White.
Mrs. Heale	Blush white.
Crown Prince	Crimson.
M. Boyer	Pink.
October Beauty	Blush.
Puritan	Blush.
Pelican	White.
Mrs. Robert Elliott	Yellow.
Grandiflorum	Yellow.
John Thorpe	Amaranth.
Jean d'Arc	Blush.
Gloriosum	Yellow.
Mrs. John Wanamaker	Lilac.
Gold	Yellow.
R. Crawford, Jr	Pink.
Peter the Great	Yellow.
La Triomphante	Rose.
Lord Mayor	Violet.
Lambeth	White.
Louis Weille	Mauve.
Robert Bottomley	White.
Venus	Blush.
William Robinson	Golden bronze.
William M. Singerly	Purple.
Leopard	Spotted.

Name.	Color.
W. W. Coles	Red.
Troubadour	Pink.
Nymphæa	White.
Lucretia	Cream.
Mrs. Carnegie	Red.
Lilian B. Bird	Pink.
Empress of India	White.
L. Canning	White.
Mrs. Langtry	White.
Mrs. Vannaman	Red.
Mrs. J. C. Price	Yellow.
Lady Matheson	Cream white.
Little Tycoon	Rose.
William H. Lincoln	Yellow.
Judge Rea	Pink.
The Bride	White.

Forty-eight of the best Japanese varieties, suitable for exhibition flowers :

Baronne de Prailly	Pink.
J. Delaux	Crimson.
Mrs. Mary Weightman	Yellow.
Comte de Germiny	Bronze.
Mrs. C. H. Wheeler	Orange red.
Mad. C. Audiguier	Pink.
Domination	White.
Mrs. Frank Thomson	Pink.
G. F. Moseman	Terra cotta.
George Maclure	Amaranth.
Grandiflorum	Yellow.
Mrs. Winthrop Sargeant	Yellow.
John Thorpe	Amaranth.
Mrs. J. N. Gerard	Pink.
Mrs. A. Waterer	White.
J. Mahood	Yellow.
La Triomphante	Rose.
Le Dauphinois	Chrome.
Le Tonkin	Pink.
Mrs. Langtry	White.
Lord Byron	Bronze.
Mrs. George Bullock	White.

Name.	Color.
Magnet	Pink.
Martha Harding	Old gold.
W. H. Lincoln	Yellow.
Pelican.	White.
Public Ledger	Pearl pink.
President Arthur	Pink.
R. Brocklebank	Yellow.
R. Crawford, Jr.	Pink.
Syringa	Peach.
Thomas Cartledge	Buff.
Charles Pratt	Claret.
Soliel Levant	Yellow.
Lady Lawrence	White.
Miss Mary Wheeler	Pink.
Mrs. T. H. Spaulding	White.
W. W. Coles.	Red.
William Robinson	Golden bronze.
H. Cannell	Yellow.
Mrs. Carnegie	Red.
Mrs. A. Hardy	White.
Lilian B. Bird	Pink.
President Spaulding	Red.
Little Tycoon	Rose.
Jessica	White.
Mrs. J. B. Wilson	Light.
The Bride	White.

Twenty-four of the best Japanese varieties, suitable for exhibition blooms :

Comte de Germiny	Bronze.
Mrs. C. H. Wheeler	Orange red.
Domination	White.
Mrs. Charles Dissel	Pink.
G. F. Moseman	Terra cotta.
Grandiflorum	Yellow.
La Triomphante	Rose.
Mrs. Langtry	White.
Le Tonkin	Pink.
Lord Byron	Bronze.
E. G. Hill	Yellow.
President Arthur	Pink.

Name.	Color.
Robert Bottomley	White.
Thomas Cartledge	Buff.
President Harrison	Crimson.
William Robinson	Golden bronze
Harry E. Widener	Yellow.
Kioto	Yellow.
The Bride	White.
Mrs. Carnegie	Red.
President Spaulding	Red.
Mollie Bawn	White.
Lilian B. Bird	Pink.
Little Tycoon	Rose.

Twenty-four of the best varieties for bush plants, suitable for exhibition or home decorations :

Cullingfordii	Red.
Grandiflorum	Yellow.
Jean d'Arc	Blush.
Mrs. John Wanamaker	Lilac.
Gold	Yellow.
R. Crawford, Jr.	Pink.
Lord Byron	Bronze.
Montplaisant	Crimson.
M. Boyer	Pink.
Puritan	Blush.
Mrs. Langtry	White.
Robert Bottomley	White.
Venus	Blush.
William Robinson	Golden bronze.
William M. Singerly	Purple.
Mrs. R. Elliott	Yellow.
Mrs. A. Hardy	White.
Mrs. Carnegie	Red.
The Bride	White.
La Triomphante	Pink.
Empress of India	White.
Gloriosum	Yellow.
Mrs. Vannaman	Red.
Judge Rea	Pink.

Twenty-four of the best Chinese varieties, suitable for exhibition blooms :

Name.	Color.
Alfred Salter	Rose pink.
Bronze Jardin des Plantes	Bronze.
Bronze Queen of England	Bronze.
Cullingfordii	Red.
Empress of India	White.
Emily Dale	Yellow.
Miss E. A. Jacquith	Bronze.
Golden Empress	Yellow.
Golden Queen of England	Yellow.
Jardin des Plantes	Yellow.
Jean d'Arc	White.
John Salter	Bronze.
Mrs. John Wanamaker	Lilac.
Lord Wolseley	Bronze red.
Lady Carey	Rose.
Mrs. M. Morgan	Light pink.
Mrs. Heale	Blush white.
M. Brunlees	Indian red.
Mabel Ward	Yellow.
Nil Desperandum	Orange.
Lady Slade	Pink.
Prince Albert	Crimson.
Princess Teck	White blush.
Sir S. Carey	Amaranth.

Twelve of the best varieties for bush plants, suitable for exhibition or conservatory decoration :

Cullingfordii	Red.
Grandiflorum	Yellow.
Mrs. John Wanamaker	Lilac.
Gold	Yellow.
M. Boyer	Pink.
Puritan	Blush.
Mrs. Robert Elliott	Yellow.
Mrs. Langtry	White.
Nymphea	White.
Montgolfier	Bronze.
Mrs. Carnegie	Red.
Lady St. Clair	White.

Twelve of the best Japanese varieties, suitable for exhibition blooms :

Name.   Color.

Comte de Germiny ....Bronze.
Etoile de Lyon ....Lilac rose.
G. F. Moseman ....Terra cotta.
Grandiflorum ....Yellow.
Mrs. Langtry ....White.
Harry E. Widener ....Yellow.
Mrs. J. T. Emlen.....................................Crimson.
Robert Bottomley ....White.
The Bride ....White.
Avalanche ....White.
Mrs. Carnegie ....Red.
Lilian B. Bird ....Pink.

Twelve of the best varieties, suitable for growing as standards :

Comte de Germiny ....Bronze.
Duchess ....Red.
Mrs. Frank Thomson...................................Pink.
G. F. Moseman ....Terra cotta.
Gold ....Yellow.
Jean d'Arc...Blush.
Grandiflorum ....Yellow.
R. Crawford, Jr ....Pink.
Robert Bottomley ....White.
Mrs. J. B. Wilson ....White.
Mrs. Carnegie ....Red.
Mad. C. Audiguier ....Pink.

Twelve of the best Anemone-flowered varieties, suitable for exhibition blooms :

Eva ....Salmon.
Empress..Lilac.
George Sand...Bronze.
Mrs. Judge Benedict ....White.
Lividia ....Blush.
M. B. Pigmy...Rose.
Nouvelle Alveole......................................Pink.
Gladys Spaulding ....Bronze.
Thorpe, Jr..Yellow.
Mrs. Charles Pratt ....White.
Fabian de Mediana....................................Lilac.
Soeur Souille ....Blush white.

Twelve of the best Chinese varieties, suitable for exhibition blooms :

Name.	Color.
Bronze Queen of England	Bronze.
Cullingfordii	Red.
Empress of India	White.
Emily Dale	Yellow.
Jean d'Arc	Blush.
Jardin des Plantes	Yellow.
Mrs. John Wanamaker	Lilac.
Lord Wolseley	Bronze red.
Mrs. Heale	Blush white.
Prince Alfred	Crimson.
Princess Teck	Violet blush.
M. Brunlees	Indian red.

CHAPTER XI.

Calendar of Monthly Operations.

JANUARY.

THE operations of this month are probably the least of any month in the year. Those who require a large number of plants will of course put in every cutting possible. Where only a few plants are required, thin out the suckers, as they appear, to the number desired from each plant. Encourage by a little liquid manure so as to get strong cuttings early next month. Towards the end of the month some of the stronger cuttings inserted in December will be rooted, and will need potting off, and should then be kept close to the glass to prevent a spindling growth. Prepare a compost of turfy loam, well rotted manure and sand ; screen, or break it up fine, as it will be required for small pots. Where good cuttings are scarce, stout suckers can be obtained with a few rootlets attached ; pot off singly and keep close until they commence to start, when plenty of ventilation can be given.

FEBRUARY.

All cuttings inserted in December will be ready for potting this month. Use two and a-half inch pots and the soil prepared last month. Examine the cuttings, and if any eyes are found on the stem that will be below the soil, they should be

(118)

rubbed off, or they will throw up suckers which will rob the main stem of its nourishment. The chief batch of cuttings should be inserted this month, and close attention paid to those already in, and the potting of those requiring it. Towards the end of the month, many will require shifting into three and a-half inch pots.

The soil for this potting should be good fibrous loam or rotted sod, with a little sand and leaf-mold added.

Chrysanthemum seed may also be sown this month in pans or boxes, in slight bottom heat until the seedlings appear. As soon as they appear, however, they should be placed close to the glass on a shelf in the greenhouse or pit. If the green fly appears, dust with snuff or tobacco powder. A still better plan is to spread some tobacco stems or refuse from the to-bacco factories upon the benches and among the plants, as the fumes from this will keep the fly away.

MARCH.

During this month many things will need attention. Most of the cuttings inserted in February will need potting and many of them will require shifting into larger pots. Have all the pots clean, especially on the inside, using a small piece of crock in each pot of four-inch size and larger, and have the soil rich and of such material as has been advised. Examine plants already potted, and if a vigorous growth has commenced, stop them by nipping out the bud in the centre of the shoot when bush plants are desired, but if standards are wanted the side buds must be rubbed out, and the main shoot encouraged in every way possible. Give abundance of air and never let them become dry or pot-bound. The only secret in their cultivation is to keep up a vigorous growth from early spring until they are in bloom in your conservatory or upon the stage of an exhibition hall. Continue propagating throughout this month, securing all the cuttings possible of rare sorts and as many as are needed of other varieties.

About the end of the month the early sown seedlings will re·
quire potting from the seed boxes or pans using the two and a
half inch pots, and after potting keep near the light but
shade from the bright sun, until they are thoroughly established.
Keep the houses in which the established plants are growing
very cool, but give all the sunshine possible. Frost, of course,
must never be allowed to enter. In the southern states, from
this time on the plants will do best in cold frames, without
artificial heat, until the time of planting out.

APRIL.

Keep a close watch upon the cuttings all this month; get
as many in as are required, pot up all that are rooted, and
keep moving into larger pots as the growth of the plants demand it. Most of the plants rooted in February and earlier
will now be in six-inch pots. The stronger growing varieties
will require a little larger pots than the more delicate sorts.
The soil must now be richer than for previous potting, using
about three parts of well rotted loam of a sandy nature, one
part of well decayed manure, and a six inch pot-full each of
bone meal and finely-broken charcoal to a bushel of this compost. Abundance of air must be given this month in the
houses where chrysanthemums are grown. Where good cold
frames are at hand all plants will be better in them than in the
houses, syringing in the evenings after hot days. Attend carefully to stopping and training. The plants intended for specimens must all be selected this month and their training be-
gun. Always have duplicate plants when growing for exhibition ; if you want to show twenty-five plants start fifty for
that purpose, and by the time the shows take place, you may
be able to select from the fifty, the twenty-five needed for exhibition. If room and the conveniences are at hand it is even
better to start with one hundred. So many accidents and dis-
appointments occur that it is best to make liberal allowances
for them. Prepare beds and borders out of doors, where

plants are to stand during the summer. In the south all the old plants should be taken up this month and divided, replanting where desired. Plants standing in cold frames or out of doors should be placed upon boards or coal ashes to prevent the worms from entering the pots. Keep also a sharp lookout for the little black fly that is so prone to infest them. If syringed a few times a week with clear soot water, it will keep them away and give the foliage a vigorous appearance.

MAY.

Many varieties, especially the pompons, may yet be rooted, all making convenient plants in the fall for decorative purposes. Plants should all be in the open air by this time, those in pots standing upon ashes or boards as recommended. All plants not intended for pot culture must be now planted out in a place prepared for them as has been directed. Place a stout stake to each plant and secure it with some strong material. Attend to the watering carefully after setting out until the plants have taken hold in the soil. Specimen plants should be in about eight inch pots at this time ; do not be in a hurry to get them into their flowering pots ; give a little weak liquid manure as soon as the plants are making a vigorous growth. By cutting back a few plants at this season to six or eight inches in height they will develop in season for late-flowering, and by cutting back a few every week until the middle of July, a succession of them may be had. If large blooms are desired the shoots must not be stopped, but allowed to grow unchecked. Select a shoot for each bloom to be grown on a plant, put a firm stake to it, and nip away all suckers and side shoots as they appear. Seedlings should also be potted as they advance in growth. Prepare a compost heap for the final potting into their flowering pots and see that a sufficient stock of suitable pots is at hand, and have them washed and put in readiness for the operation. Prepare tanks or barrels for liquid manure, and stakes and wire for training.

JUNE.

The principal duty of this month is the transferring of the plants into larger pots, and many of the most vigorous plants that are of good size may be put into their blooming pots. Many, however, that were propagated late must not be put into their blooming pots until July. The final potting is of the utmost importance, as the ultimate success depends in no small degree upon this operation. The soil for this purpose is described elsewhere in this book, and the pots should be from nine to twelve inches in diameter for the last change. The stopping of all plants in the borders should be continued; always having in mind the desired shape of the plant, in the pinching of the shoots. The tying of all specimens must be given close attention through this month, as a good foundation for all specimen plants must be laid early in July. Tie down and spread out all long shoots, being careful not to snap them off in the operation. The safest way is to tie a piece of string or matting from the shoot you intend to tie down, to the main stem. When the shoot is then bent the strain comes on the string and not on the tender union of shoot to the main branch. In potting do not fill the pots too full of soil; leave room for a top dressing of cow manure in August. Those not quite ready for their blooming pots will require liquid manure; and the entire lot careful watering, frequent syringing, and a sharp lookout for insect pests.

JULY.

Plants growing out of doors in the open ground without pots must have plenty of water, and the surface not allowed to become hard and baked. A working with a rake, or pronged hoe, will prevent this if repeated every week. In a very dry time a mulch of manure will prevent them from drying out so rapidly. The July bud will now be appearing on most varieties on the points of the strongest and earliest shoots, and must be carefully removed at once. Two or three shoots will appear from below, and the terminal bud on each one of these shoots will produce fine blooms. All plants should be put into the pots in which they are to bloom this month, and the tying, watering, syringing and looking after the insects all closely attended to. Specimen plants should be set a suitable distance apart, and plunged about two thirds the depth of the pots into coal ashes or other material that will prevent the influence of the sun from reaching them and drying them out. Plants which are to bloom in November should not be stopped after this month ; such varieties as Grandiflorum should not be stopped after the first of the month. Syringe the plants occasionally with quassia water. Do not pot and stop the plants at the same time, as each repotting at once sets the roots into active growth, and the growth of the top is checked for a time. Wait until you see signs of renewed growth, after repotting, before you begin to stop. Cuttings can be rooted this month, but do not root as readily as in spring. Young plants started now make pretty objects for the pit or conservatory late in November and will bloom freely in four-inch pots.

AUGUST.

No potting will need to be done this month. The work will include a constant attention to watering chiefly, together with staking and top-dressing. Such varieties as E. H. Fitler, Mrs. W. K. Harris and Mrs. Alpheus Hardy are better indoors. A mulch of sheep or cow manure may be given this month on the tops of the pots during hot weather. If the pots are too full of soil to admit of a sufficient dressing, the manure can be banked up around the edge of the pot so as to preserve a basin on top to hold the water. About the end of this month the flower buds will begin to appear at the end of the strong young shoots. Beneath each terminal bud will be noticed three or four prominent buds growing from the axils of the leaves, immediately beneath the flower bud. These side shoots, if allowed to remain, would draw considerably from the nutriment of the bud, and on this account must be carefully removed. After their removal, the flowering buds begin to swell rapidly, and liberal applications of liquid manure must be made. If the buds appear early in August, it is best to rub them out and let another shoot come and produce another bud which will undoubtedly give the best bloom. The crown or terminal bud that forms early in August will not as a rule make a good bloom, being liable to be deformed. Any buds that appear after the last week in August may be retained, as all will make good blooms that form after that date. A variety of liquid manures should be on hand all through this and the next two months, so as to give the plants a change occasionally, which is highly beneficial.

SEPTEMBER.

Where large blooms are required, disbudding should be closely attended to all through this month, and the tying and training of specimen plants should receive the undivided attention of every cultivator. Watering, top-dressing and syringing are also important points now. Nearly all the varieties will be showing their buds by the middle of the month, and these must be thinned out in accordance with the purpose of the grower. The top-dressing must be resorted to in wet weather, as the rain carries the fertility down to the roots. Manure water cannot be advantageously applied when the weather is very wet, and the top-dressing is the best way to furnish them their nourishment. At this time it may be piled a couple of inches above the rim of the pot, leaving a basin in the center to hold water. All plants intended for indoor decoration that have been growing in the open ground during the summer, should now be taken up and potted. Shade well for a few days, keeping them sprinkled, and gradually inure them to the full sunlight. Stake carefully, and remove only leaves that have wilted and become brown during the operation.

OCTOBER.

In the operations for this month much depends on the locality. In northern latitudes all plants would have to be in their flowering quarters by the first of the month, or earlier ; while in more favored localities, the middle of this month is a good time to move the plants indoors. By the end of September or first few days of October, all shoots and flower buds should be tied for the last time in the position in which it is desired to have them remain. This gives them a few weeks to turn up and assume a more natural style of growth, than when tied in place a few days prior to the exhibition. Keep the house in which they are grown well ventilated, and allow no surplus water to remain on the floors over night. The disbudding must not be forgotten all through this month, as little shoots and buds will be forming constantly on all the main stems, to the detriment of the blooms unless speedily removed. The plants should by this time become thoroughly accustomed to the liquid manure, and it should now be given stronger and more frequently, as there will be a great draft on the vital resources of the plant at this time in developing its blooms. Mildew must be looked after carefully and kept in check by abundant ventilation, and in case of extremely dull weather a little fire heat will be beneficial. Should mildew appear, dust with flour sulphur upon the affected parts. When housing the plants, if it is necessary to have all in bloom at the same time, shade may be given to the earlier sorts, while the more tardy varieties should be exposed to the full sunlight. A few light fumigations after the flowers are placed in their quarters will entirely rid them of the fly, if there should be any remaining upon them, and they will then be in a clean healthy condition to come into bloom. Plants grown out of doors in the South will require attention at this time. Preparations should be made to protect them from the first frosts, as in this section there are usually a few light frosts about the 20th of the month.   If protected from these they may continue blooming for a month, and be very beautiful objects through early November.

NOVEMBER.

Liquid manure must be withheld as the flowers expand. Give each plant as much room as possible, and arrange the plants to the best advantage for displaying their blooms. From the beginning of the month most of them will be in bloom, and but little more remains to be done in regard to cultivation.   Careful watering, a brisk, dry atmosphere, and abundance of ventilation alone are necessary.   It is now a good time to go through and see that all kinds are correctly labeled, making observations and taking notes for future reference.

DECEMBER.

Plants that are through blooming should be cut down, leaving one or two of the growing branches, as, if entirely cut down to the soil, cuttings will not be produced freely and weak or tender sorts would be liable to succumb entirely. In taking out the stakes fill the holes up with soil, in order to prevent the water running through without becoming distributed through the soil.   Some growers insert many cuttings this month, and when this is deemed necessary, the work should be proceeded with at once.

Many little defects will perhaps be observed by the studious grower in his selection of varieties at this season, and other improvements will doubtless here and there suggest themselves: so, with new purposes and firm resolves he starts out on the succeeding season's work before the present season is ended.

Copyright 1889
by F. R. PIERSON.

JAPANESE

5
2
4

"The Queen of Autumn"

CHRYSANTHEMUMS

We have undoubtedly the most charming novelties in this flower ever introduced, and we are constantly adding to our collection the rarest and best introductions of the noted raisers of America, Europe and Japan, winners of the **First Prize,** and receiving the highest honors **wherever exhibited.** A revelation to all who have seen them. They are so elegant that we wholesale the single flowers for twenty-five cents each, which will give some idea of their choiceness. **These are fully described in our large illustrated Catalogue of all the BEST NEW SEEDS AND PLANTS.** It is very complete, handsomely illustrated, artistic, of particular interest to all lovers of choice flowers. Sent free to all readers of this book enclosing stamp to pay postage. Address, mentioning "Chrysanthemum Culture,"

P. O. BOX 25

F. R. PIERSON, FLORIST AND SEEDSMAN, TARRYTOWN, N.Y.

HORTICULTURIST'S RULE-BOOK.

Designed as a pocket companion. The book has been prepared with great care and much labor. It contains in handy and concise form a great number of the rules and receipts required by fruit-growers, truck gardeners, florists, farmers, etc. Undoubtedly the best thing of the kind ever published.

BY L. H. BAILEY,

Editor of The American Garden, Horticulturist of the Cornell Experiment Station and Professor of Horticulture in Cornell University.

CONTENTS OF THE BOOK.

I. **Insecticides.**

II. **Injurious insects,** with preventives and remedies.

III. **Fungicides** for plant diseases.

IV. **Plant diseases,** with preventives and remedies.

V. **Injuries** from mice, rabbits, birds, etc., with preventives and remedies.

VI. **Weeds.**

VII. **Waxes and washes** for grafting and for wounds.

VIII. **Cements, paints,** etc.

IX. **Seed Tables:** 1. Quantities required for sowing given areas 2. Weight and size of seeds of kitchen garden vegetables. 3. Longevity of seeds. 4. Time required for kitchen garden seeds to germinate.

X. **Planting Tables:** 1. Dates for sowing or setting kitchen garden vegetables in different latitudes. 2. Tender and hardy vegetables 3. Usual distances apart for planting fruits and vegetables. 4. Number of plants required to set an acre at given distances apart.

XI. **Maturity and Yields:** 1. Time required for the maturity of kitchen garden vegetables. 2. Time required for the bearing of fruit plants. 3. Longevity of fruit plants. 4. Average yields of various crops.

XII. **Methods of keeping and storing** fruits and vegetables.

XIII. **Multiplication and Propagation of Plants:** 1. Methods of multiplying plants. 2. Ways of grafting and budding. 3. Particular methods by which various fruits are propagated. 4. Stocks used for various fruits.

XIV. **Standard Measures and Sizes:** 1. Standard flower pots. 2. Standard and legal measures. 3. English measures for sale of fruits and vegetables,

XV. **Tables of weights and measures.**

XVI. **Miscellaneous** tables, figures and notes: 1. Quantities of water held in pipes and tanks. 2. Thermometer scales. 3. Effect of wind in cooling glass roofs. 4. Per cent. of light reflected from glass at various angles of inclination. 5. Weights of various varieties of apples per bushel. 6. Amount of various products yielded by given quantities of fruit. 7. Labels. 8. Miscellany.

XVII. **Rules:** 1. Loudon's rules of horticulture. 2. Rules of nomenclature. 3. Rules for exhibition.

XVIII. **Postal rates and regulations.**

XIX. **Weather signs,** and protection from frost.

XX. **Collecting and preserving :** 1. How to make an herbarium. 2. Preserving and printing of flowers and other parts of plants. 3. Keeping cut-flowers. 4. Perfumery. 5. How to collect and preserve insects.

XXI. **Elements, symbols and analyses:** 1. The elements and their chemical symbols. 2. Chemical composition of a few common substances. Analyses: (*a*) Fruits and Vegetables; (*b*) Seeds and Fertilizers; (*c*) Soils and Minerals.

XXII. **Names and histories :** 1. Vegetables which have different names in England and America. 2. Derivation of names of various fruits and vegetables. 3. Names of fruits and vegetables in various languages. 4. Periods of cultivation and native countries of cultivated plants.

XVIII. **Facts and statistics** of horticulture and the vegetable kingdom.

XXIV. **Glossary** of technical words used by horticulturists.

XXV. **Calendar.**

Price in library style cloth, wide margins, **$1**; pocket style, paper, narrow margins, **50 cts.**

THE RURAL PUBLISHING COMPANY, Times Building, N. Y.

THE NURSERY BOOK

A Complete Hand-Book of Propagation and Pollination.

By L. H. BAILEY.

Uniform in Size and Style with Rule-Book of 1890 Edition. Illustrated.

This valuable little manual has been compiled at great pains. The author has had unusual facilities for its preparation, having been aided by many experts in many directions.

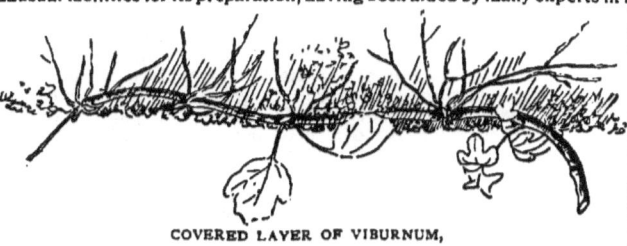

The book is absolutely devoid of theory and speculation. It has nothing to do with plant physiology, nor with any obtruse reasons of plant growth. It simply tells plainly and briefly what everyone who sows a

COVERED LAYER OF VIBURNUM,

seed, makes a cutting, sets a graft, or crosses a flower wants to know. It is entirely new and original in method and matter. The cuts number almost 100, and are made especially for it, direct from nature. The book treats all kinds of cultivated plants, fruits, vegetables, greenhouse plants, hardy herbs, ornamental trees and shrubs, forest trees.

CONTENTS.

Chapter I.—**Seedage.** Chapter II.—**Separation and |Division.** Chapter III.— **Layerage.** Chapter IV.—**Cuttage.** |Chapter V.—**Graftage.** Including Grafting, Budding, Inarching, etc.

Chapter VI.—**Nursery List.**

This is the great feature of the book. It has an alphabetical list of all kinds of plants, with a short statement telling which of the operations described in the first five chapters are employed in propagating them. **Over 2,000 entries** are made in the list. The following entries will give an idea of the method:

ACER (Maple). *Sapindaceæ.* Stocks are grown from stratified seeds, which should be sown an inch or two deep; or some species, as *A. dasycarpum*, come readily if seeds are simply sown as soon as ripe. Some cultural varieties are layered, but better plants are obtained by grafting. Varieties of native species are worked upon common or native stocks. The Japanese sorts are winter-worked upon imported *A. polymorphum* stocks, either by whip or veneer-grafting. Maples can also be budded in summer, and they grow readily from cuttings of both ripe and soft wood.

PHYLLOCACTUS, PHYLLOCEREUS, DISOCACTUS (Leaf-Cactus). *Cacteæ.* Fresh seeds grow readily. Sow in rather sandy soil, which is well drained, and apply water as for common seeds. When the seedlings appear, remove to a light position. Cuttings from mature shoots, three to six inches in length. root readily in sharp sand. Give a temperature of about 60°, and apply only sufficient water to keep from flagging. If the cuttings are very juicy, they may be laid on dry sand for several days before planting.

GOOSEBERRY. Seeds, for the raising of new varieties should be sown as soon as well cured, in loam or sandy soil, or they may be stratified and sown together well with the sand in the spring. Cuttings six to eight inches long, of the mature wood, inserted two-thirds their length, usually grow readily, especially if taken in August or September and stored during winter. Stronger plants are usually obtained by layers, and the English varieties are nearly always layered in this country. Mound-layering is usually employed, th · English varieties being allowed to remain in layerage two years, but the American varieties only one (Fig. 27). Layerage plants are usually set in nursery rows for a year after removal from the stools. Green-layering during summer is sometimes practised for new or rare varieties.

Chapter VII.—**Pollination,** giving directions for making crosses, etc.

This book is now completed, and is on sale. Price, in library style, cloth, wide margins, $1; Pocket style, paper, narrow margins, **50 cents.**

THE RURAL PUBLISHING CO., Times Building, New York.

The New Potato Culture

By ELBERT S. CARMAN,

Editor of THE RURAL NEW-YORKER.

This book will give the results of the author's investigations and experiments during the past fifteen years. Its object will be to show all who raise potatoes, whether for home use solely or for market as well, that the yield may be increased threefold without a corresponding increase in the cost; to show that the little garden patch, of a fortieth of an acre perhaps, may just as well yield ten bushels as three bushels: to induce farmers and gardeners to experiment with fertilizers not only as to the kind, that is to say, the constituents and their most effective proportions, but as to the most economical quantity to use; to experiment as to the most telling preparation of the soil, the depth to plant, the size of seed, the number or eyes, the distance apart. These will be among the subjects considered, not in a theoretical way at all, but as the outcome of fifteen years of experimentation earnestly made in the hope of advancing our knowledge of this mighty industry. It is respectfully submitted that these experiments so long carried on at the Rural Grounds have, directly and indirectly, thrown more light upon the various problems involved in successful potato culture, than any other experiments which have been carried on in America. **Price, Cloth, 75 Cents ; Paper, 40 Cents.**

THE RURAL PUBLISHING COMPANY, Times Building, New York.

Annals of Horticulture for 1890.

By Professor L. H. Bailey.

As a work of reference for all students of plants and nature, this

will be invaluable. No one who expects to keep up with the progress of the times can be without it. An especial feature of the volume for 1890 will be a census of cultivated plants of American origin, with dates of introduction and extent of variation under culture. This includes all ornamentals and all esculents, and will include hundreds of entries. It will form an invaluable contribution to the knowledge of the origin and variation of plants. The novelties of 1890, tools and convenience of the year, directories, lists of plant portraits, including all the leading journals of the world this year, recent horticultural literature, and other chapters, are each alone worth many times more than the cost of the book. What have horticulturists thought about during 1890? This is the theme of the book.

Profusely Illustrated. Iu full cloth, $1 ; Paper 60 cents.
THE RURAL PUBLISHING CO., Times Building, New York.

What is
The Rural New-Yorker?

The MOST TRUSTWORTHY of any paper of its class printed.—J. J. Harrison, President of the Storrs & Harrison Company.

Everybody that *is* a body knows of the UNIQUE INDIVIDUALITY of the Rural along the lines of original experimental investigation.—J. J. H. Gregory.

The editor of the Rural New-Yorker has opened an entirely NEW FIELD OF INVESTIGATION, the possibilities of which cannot be conjectured.—Norman J. Colman.

The Rural New-Yorker has DONE MORE FOR FARMERS than nine-tenth of all the land-grant colleges and Experiment stations.—*New York Tribune.*

We have seen on the farm of the editor of The Rural New-Yorker a crop of 134 bushels of shelled corn raised on one acre of land.—*American Agriculturist.*

The Rural New-Yorker illustrates the PROGRESS made by the agricultural class, much of which is due to the inspiration of The Rural New-Yorker, and the papers which follow its example.—Lt. Gov. E. F. Jones.

The Rural New-Yorker has DONE MORE TO PROMOTE THE TRUE INTERESTS OF AGRICULTURE than all the Experiment Stations put together.—*The New York Times.*

The best farm weekly in the world.—*Farm Journal.*

$2.00 a year. On trial, ten weeks, 25 cents.

THE RURAL PUBLISHING COMPANY, Times Building, New York.

☞ANYTHING THAT YOU WANT, no matter what, at REDUCED COST, in return for sending us clubs of subscriptions.